CROSS STITCH
INSPIRATIONS

dear God be good
to me, my boat is
so small and the
sea so wide...
FISHERMAN'S PRAYER

CROSS STITCH
INSPIRATIONS

27 DESIGNS FROM PSALMS AND VERSES

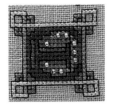

SUE COOK

David & Charles

'For Ade - with my love and thanks - Susie'

Detail from the Spring Hanging Banner

A DAVID & CHARLES BOOK

First published in the UK in 1999

Text and designs Copyright © Sue Cook 1999
Photography and layout Copyright © David & Charles 1999

A catalogue record for this book is available from the British Library.

ISBN 0 7153 0798 3

Photography by David Johnson
Styling by Kit Johnson
Book design by Diana Knapp
Edited by Juliet Bracken
and printed in Italy by LEGO SpA
for David & Charles
Brunel House   Newton Abbot   Devon

Contents

To Everything There is a Season

*'To everything there is a season and a time
for every purpose under Heaven'*

ECCLESIASTES, 3:1

This well-known Old Testament verse seemed the perfect way to open a book celebrating not only the pleasures of the passing seasons but the whole cycle of life itself. On the following pages you will find designs inspired by such simple joys as gardening and homemaking, as well as the pleasure of friendship. Birth, marriage, retirement and the contentment of old age – in fact all the milestones of life – are to be found here. I hope this book will give a sense of my own personal belief that all of us have a part to play, however small, in the greater scheme of things. Nothing illustrates this better than our desire to leave a lasting legacy to future generations with our lovingly-created cross stitch. So begin your creative journey here, within the shelter of this little walled garden. Watch Spring blossom into high Summer, followed by the gold of Autumn and the long quiet night of Winter. Like the garden, the gardener moves from beginning to end and back to the beginning again, following life's eternal circle.
A time for every purpose.

◆

DESIGN SIZE: 6⅝ x 10⅛in (17 x 25.5cm)
STITCH COUNT: 93 wide x 142 high

◆

YOU WILL NEED

* Cream 14-count aida, 14 x 16in (35.5 x 40.5cm)
* DMC stranded cotton (floss) as listed in the key
* Tapestry needle, size 24
* DMC seed beads, V1.04.809, Sky blue
* Mount board, 12 x 14in (30.5 x 35.5cm)
* Picture frame of your choice

1 Find the centre of your fabric by folding it in half first lengthways and then widthways. Mark the folds with two lines of tacking (basting) stitches if desired. Count away from this point on both your fabric and the 'To Everything There is a Season' chart on pages 8–9, then begin stitching the backstitch lettering using one strand of cotton (floss). Check that you have positioned it correctly before starting to work the cross stitch.

2 Use two strands of cotton (floss) for the cross stitch, except for those areas that are stitched in one strand to add depth to the design (for example, the cloud on the top border). These are listed with a separate symbol in the key. Use one strand of cotton (floss) for all the other backstitch on the design as well, and one strand for the French knots.

3 When the cross stitch is complete, attach each of the beads with a half cross (see page 125) following the chart.

4 The wands held by the two cherubs are long stitches worked in two strands across the front of the design. Refer to the chart for their placement.

5 Wash and press your finished work and prepare it for framing (see page 126).

To everything
there is a season
and a time
for every purpose
under Heaven

Ecclesiastes 3:1

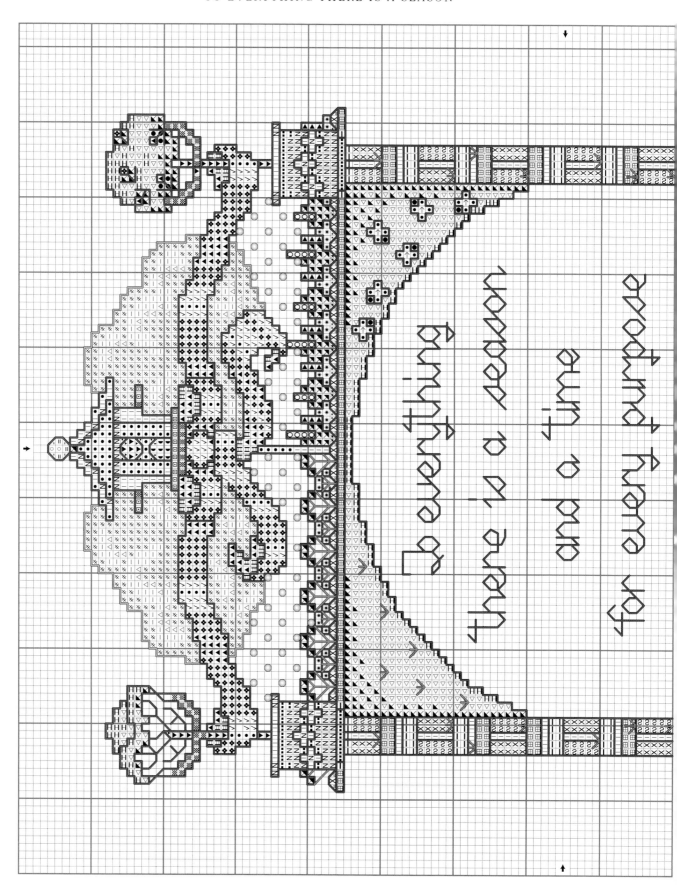

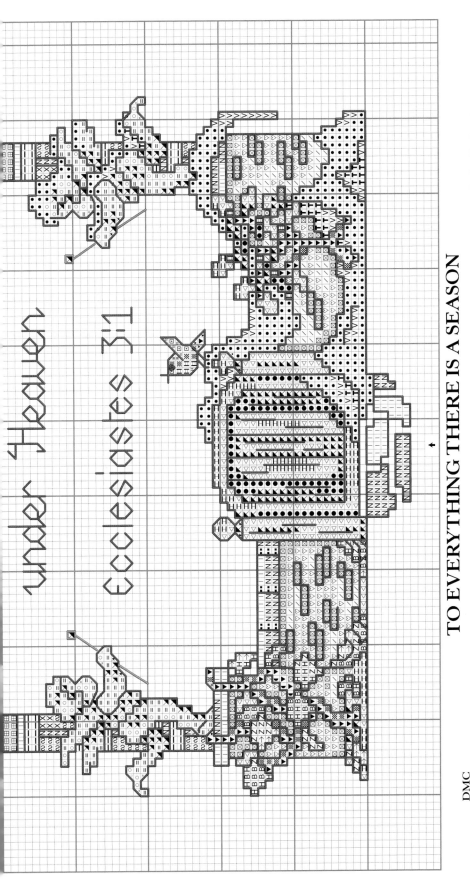

TO EVERYTHING THERE IS A SEASON

DMC
Cross stitch

·	01	White
✗	3823	Yellow - v pale (1)
−	01	White (1)
△	341	Blue Violet - lt (1)
⊞	301	Mahogany - med
T	341	Blue Violet - lt
H	350	Peach - med
▲	351	Peach
✓	352	Peach - lt
−	353	Peach - v lt
X	400	Mahogany - dk
X	402	Mahogany - v lt
▓	433	Brown Golden - dk
⊡	435	Brown Golden - v lt
◤	469	Avocado Green
▽	470	Avocado Green - lt
H	471	Avocado Green - v lt
✶	501	Blue Green - dk
◥	502	Blue Green
◯	504	Blue Green - lt
▲	553	Violet
◯◯	554	Violet - lt
⊠	611	Drab Brown
⟋	612	Drab Brown - lt
▷▷	613	Drab Brown - v lt
···	646	Beaver Grey - dk
N	647	Beaver Grey - med
⫼	648	Beaver Grey - lt
H	741	Tangerine - med
→→	743	Yellow - med
▶▶	801	Coffee Brown - dk
◆▶	898	Coffee Brown - v dk
B	920	Copper - med
Z	922	Copper - lt
●●	936	Avocado Green - dk
V	3747	Blue Violet - v lt
◐◐	3776	Mahogany - lt.
=	3813	Blue Green - lt

Backstitch
—	341	Blue Violet - lt
—	469	Avocado Green
—	502	Blue Green
—	838	Beige Brown - v dk

French knot
●	898	Coffee Brown - v dk

Beads
◯	DMC seed beads	
	V1. 04.809 Sky Blue	

STITCH NOTES

Stitched on 14-count aida using two strands for cross stitch unless indicated when the number of strands is listed in brackets. Long stitch in two strands. Backstitch in one strand. Attach beads with a half cross.

Spring
BEGINNINGS

Spring – the light at the end of the dark tunnel of winter and bringer of hope. Just as nature awakens from its long slumber, so we sit up and take stock of our surroundings. We may undertake anything from a quick spring clean to a complete change of lifestyle.

This section celebrates the beginning of the cycle of life and the hope we feel as the year turns and stretches before us. And what could be more important than the gift of life itself in the precious newborn infant? Over the next few pages you'll find a series of gifts to stitch for a new arrival, including a sampler, a mobile, two keepsakes and an afghan, all decorated with mischievous cherubs and watchful angels.

Spring is the time for planting for the year ahead as tiny green shoots, survivors of the frost and winter rains, beckon us into the garden again. So for the gardener there's a set of projects with an Amish theme. The basket to hold a plant and the sturdy apron will make practical gifts. And for when it's time to sit back and admire your handiwork, there's a matching willow wreath and herb pillow.

As the promise of warmer days to come fills us with renewed energy, we may take on new projects or complete long-neglected ones. To remind us of the guiding presence in all we do, an evocative image of childhood illustrates the familiar words of the Lord's Prayer.

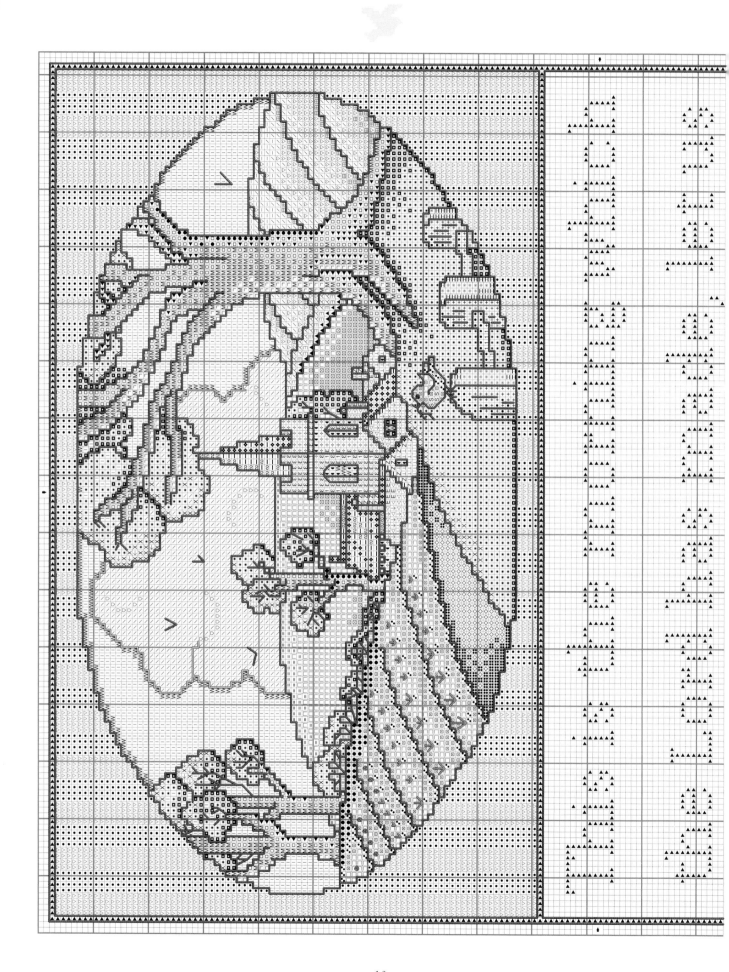

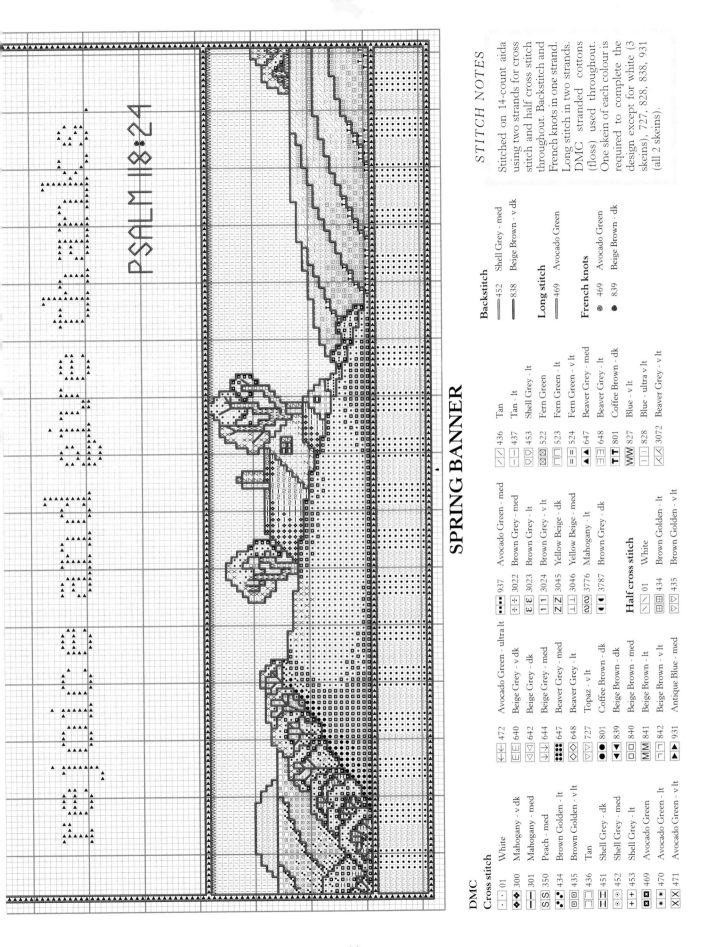

THIS IS THE DAY THE LORD HAS MADE

PSALM 118:24

SPRING BANNER

STITCH NOTES

Stitched on 14-count aida using two strands for cross stitch and half cross stitch throughout. Backstitch and French knots in one strand. Long stitch in two strands. DMC stranded cottons (floss) used throughout. One skein of each colour is required to complete the design except for white (3 skeins), 727, 828, 838, 931 (all 2 skeins).

DMC

Cross stitch

· ·	01	White
❖	300	Mahogany - v dk
−	301	Mahogany - med
S S	350	Peach - med
•:	434	Brown Golden - lt
�◨	435	Brown Golden - v lt
□	436	Tan
H H	451	Shell Grey - dk
◉ ·	452	Shell Grey - med
+ +	453	Shell Grey - lt
◧	469	Avocado Green
✳	470	Avocado Green - lt
X X	471	Avocado Green - v lt

← ←	472	Avocado Green - ultra lt
E E	640	Beige Grey - v dk
▽◁	642	Beige Grey - dk
↓↓	644	Beige Grey - med
◦◦	647	Beaver Grey - med
◇◇	648	Beaver Grey - lt
▷▽	727	Topaz - v lt
● ●	801	Coffee Brown - dk
▼	839	Beige Brown - dk
□□	840	Beige Brown - med
M M	841	Beige Brown - lt
⊤⊤	842	Beige Brown - v lt
▲▲	931	Antique Blue - med

▪▪▪	937	Avocado Green - med
÷÷	3022	Brown Grey - med
ε ε	3023	Brown Grey - lt
1 1	3024	Brown Grey - v lt
Z Z	3045	Yellow Beige - dk
⊥⊥	3046	Yellow Beige - med
⊘⊘	3776	Mahogany - lt
◀	3787	Brown Grey - dk

/ /	436	Tan
− −	437	Tan - lt
▽ ▽	453	Shell Grey - lt
⊠⊠	522	Fern Green
⊓⊓	523	Fern Green - lt
= =	524	Fern Green - v lt
▲ ▲	647	Beaver Grey - med
⊞⊞	648	Beaver Grey - lt
T T	801	Coffee Brown - dk
W W	827	Blue - v lt
⊡⊡	828	Blue - ultra v lt
X X	3072	Beaver Grey - v lt

Half cross stitch

\ \	01	White
⊞⊞	434	Brown Golden - lt
▽ ▽	435	Brown Golden - v lt

Backstitch

——	452	Shell Grey - med
——	838	Beige Brown - v dk

Long stitch

——	469	Avocado Green

French knots

◉	469	Avocado Green
●	839	Beige Brown - dk

Spring Hanging Banner

This is the first of four banners which form a running theme through the book. To give continuity, I chose to show a little village nestling in a valley. Here you will see the changing seasons unfold in each section of the book. Watch to see how the sun moves across the heavens from the bright sunrise of Spring to the low slanting shadows of a Winter twilight. To tie the banners together, they all have the same striped border and an appropriate verse to reflect the mood of the season. Where is this village? It exists in my imagination, but I like to think it is the kind of peaceful place each of us holds in our heart. Although there is a lot of stitching in this design it is very simple to work. It uses only whole cross stitches, with half stitches to add depth, and backstitch. If you find the whole project too daunting, just stitch the landscape at the top to go in a frame.

◆

DESIGN SIZE : 10¾ x 14¾in (27.5 x 37.5cm)
STITCH COUNT: 151 wide x 205 high

◆

YOU WILL NEED

* Cream 14-count aida, 15 x 18in (38 x 46cm)
* DMC stranded cotton (floss) as listed in the key
* Tapestry needle, size 24
* White cotton backing fabric, 20in (50cm)
* Silk cord, 2¼ yds (2m)
* Large wooden bell-pull or doweling and wooden knobs for hanging

1 Find the centre of your fabric by folding it in half lengthways and widthways. Start stitching from the middle of the chart on pages 12–13 using two strands of cotton (floss) for the cross stitch, and one strand for the backstitch and French knots. Parts of the design are worked in half cross stitch using two strands to create a receding background, and listed separately in the key.

2 Follow the key carefully when backstitching because several different colours are used to give the project depth.

3 The crops in the field are worked as long stitches using two strands of 469.

TO MAKE UP THE BANNER

1 Turn under and press to the wrong side a ¼in (6mm) seam around the edges of the stitched piece.

2 Cut four pieces of white cotton backing fabric, each measuring 6½ x 4½in (16.5 x 11.5cm), to make the tabs. Then, with right sides together, pin, tack (baste) and sew the long edges of each tab together in a ¼in (6mm) seam. Turn to the right side and press, keeping the seam in the centre back of the tab.

3 With the wrong side of the work facing, position the first tab on the top edge 1¼in (3cm) from the left-hand edge. Fold it in half and pin and tack (baste) both ends to the stitching, keeping the seams to the centre back. Measure the same distance from the right-hand side and pin the second tab in position. Repeat this for the two remaining tabs, ensuring they are evenly spaced. Machine or hand sew into place and press the tabs.

4 To make the backing for the banner, cut a piece of white cotton fabric measuring 15 x 18in (38 x 46cm). Fold under to the wrong side and press a ¼in (6mm) seam all round the edges.

5 With wrong sides together, place the backing on top of the stitching, pin and slip stitch all the edges neatly. Finish off by whipstitching the silk cord around the edge, starting from the centre bottom of the banner and adding a dab of clear glue to the cord ends to prevent fraying. Thread the chosen hanger through the tabs.

◆

The Darling of the World Has Come

'We see Him come and know Him ours, who with His sunshine
and His showers turns all the patient ground to flowers, the
Darling of the World has come, and it is fit we find a room to
welcome Him, the nobler part of all this house here, is the heart'

ROBERT HERRICK

This lovely verse, celebrating the most famous birth of all, is perfect for a sampler which shares the joy of a family's new arrival. Babies are so precious that we like to think they have a guardian angel who watches over them. So I drew a host of angels keeping watch over a smiling cherub with a mischievous twinkle in his eye. Flowing ribbons, bluebirds bearing a beaded garland and a gold heart charm add the finishing touches. Cherubs and angels also feature on my gifts for a new baby. These include a musical pillow, an afghan, a mobile and other keepsakes.

◆

Angels and Cherubs Birth Sampler

DESIGN SIZE: 9 x 8in (22.5 x 20cm)
STITCH COUNT: 125 high x 111 wide

◆

YOU WILL NEED

* Cream 14-count aida, 14 x 16in (35.5 x 40.5cm)
* DMC stranded cotton (floss) as listed in the key
* Kreinik Braid No. 8, 221 Gold
* DMC seed beads, 01.3779, Pale salmon; 01.503, Sea green
* Tapestry needle, size 24
* Beading needle
* Gold heart charm
* Graph paper

1 Find the centre of the fabric by folding it in half lengthways and widthways. Mark the folds with a line of tacking (basting) stitches if desired. Count away from this point both on the chart on pages 16–17 and on your fabric, and begin by stitching the bluebird garlands. Use two strands of stranded cotton (floss) for the cross stitch and one strand for the backstitch.

2 Draw your baby's name and date on a separate sheet of graph paper, spacing them like the example shown on the chart. Copy out the last few rows of the heart motif, then centre your lettering below this. When you are happy with the way it looks, stitch it on your sampler.

3 Attach a bead for each symbol marked on the chart with a half cross stitch using a beading needle threaded with one strand of matching cotton (see page 125).

4 Wait until you have completed all the stitching before attaching the gold heart charm. Wash and press the design (see page 126), then attach the charm in the position indicated on the chart with a few neat stitches using a length of Kreinik No. 8 gold braid.

5 Your sampler is now ready to be mounted for framing (see page 126).

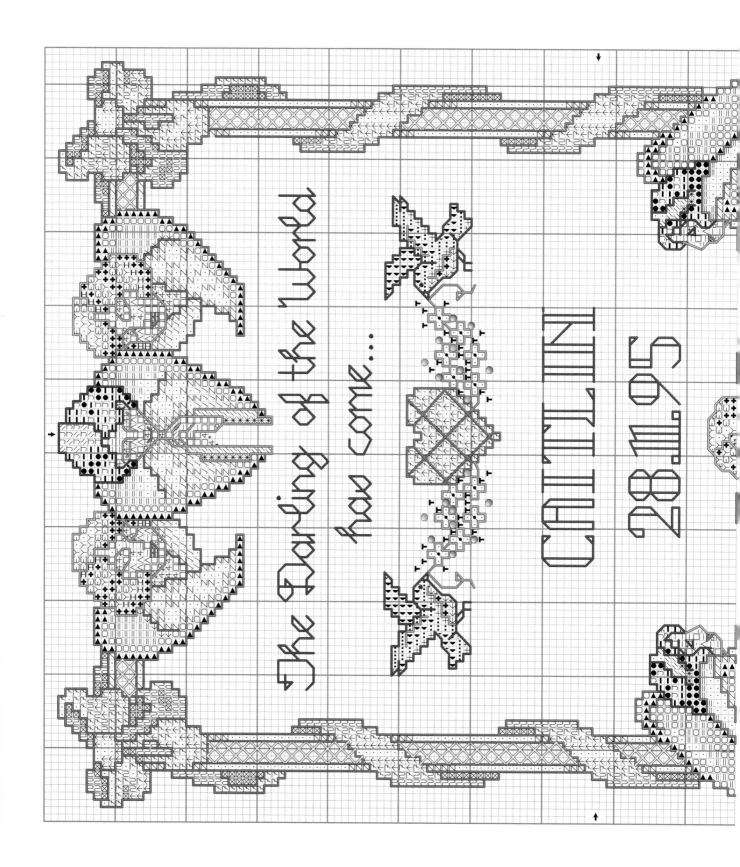

The Darling of the World

has come...

CAITLIN

28.III.95

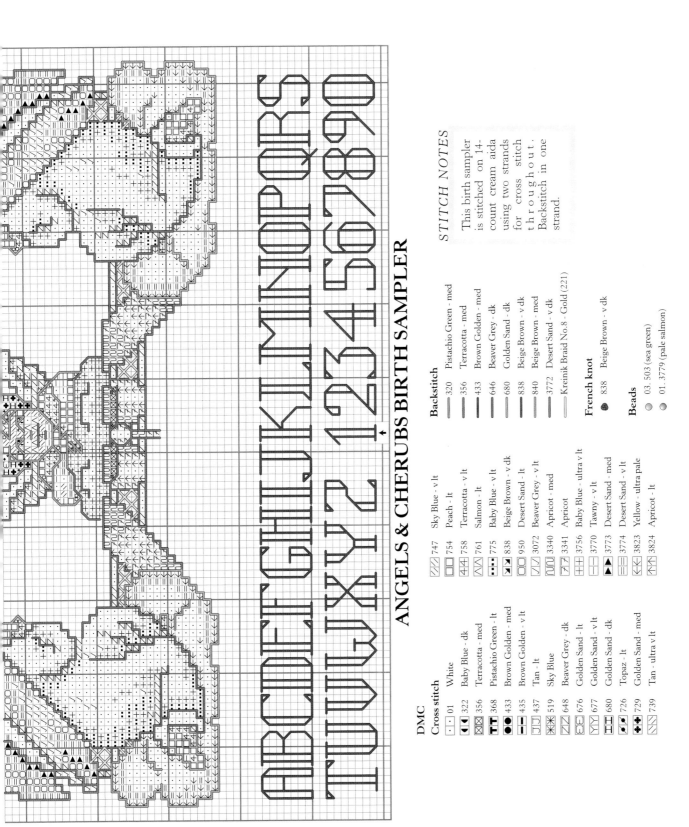

ANGELS & CHERUBS BIRTH SAMPLER

STITCH NOTES

This birth sampler is stitched on 14-count cream aida using two strands for cross stitch throughout. Backstitch in one strand.

DMC

Cross stitch

·	01	White
◀	322	Baby Blue - dk
⊠	356	Terracotta - med
T	368	Pistachio Green - lt
●	433	Brown Golden - med
—	435	Brown Golden - v lt
J	437	Tan - lt
✳	519	Sky Blue
Z	648	Beaver Grey - dk
E	676	Golden Sand - lt
Y	677	Golden Sand - v lt
H	680	Golden Sand - dk
◢	726	Topaz - lt
✚	729	Golden Sand - med
N	739	Tan - ultra v lt
Z	747	Sky Blue - v lt
□	754	Peach - lt
4	758	Terracotta - v lt
∧	761	Salmon - lt
⋯	775	Baby Blue - v lt
◥	838	Beige Brown - v dk
○	950	Desert Sand - lt
/	3072	Beaver Grey - v lt
U	3340	Apricot - med
Z	3341	Apricot
╫	3756	Baby Blue - ultra v lt
—	3770	Tawny - v lt
▲	3773	Desert Sand - med
▲	3774	Desert Sand - v lt
◀	3823	Yellow - ultra pale
Y	3824	Apricot - lt

Backstitch

—	320	Pistachio Green - med
—	356	Terracotta - med
—	433	Brown Golden - med
—	646	Beaver Grey - dk
—	680	Golden Sand - dk
—	838	Beige Brown - v dk
—	840	Beige Brown - med
—	3772	Desert Sand - v dk
—		Kreinik Braid No.8 - Gold (221)

French knot

●	838	Beige Brown - v dk

Beads

○	03.	503 (sea green)
○	01.	3779 (pale salmon)

Sweet Dreams Musical Pillow

The three watchful angels and pretty bluebirds from the sampler feature on a pale blue pillow which hides a tiny music box to soothe baby to sleep. Beautiful mother-of-pearl buttons in the shape of the crescent moon secure its hanging ribbon.

◆

DESIGN SIZE: 4¾ x 5in (12 x 12.5cm)
STITCH COUNT: 66 high x 70 wide

◆

YOU WILL NEED

* Pale blue 28-count jobelan, two 8.5 x 8.5in
(21.6 x 21.6cm) pieces
* DMC stranded cotton (floss) as listed in the key
* Sky blue 1in (2.5cm) double-faced satin ribbon, 20in (50cm)
* 2in (5cm) pre-gathered white lace, 39in (1m)
* Mother-of-pearl buttons (optional) – see safety note below
* Small music box (this must have a plastic case with a screw-in key)
* Small bag of good-quality toy filling
* Double-sided tape

1 Find the centre of one of the pieces of jobelan by folding it in half lengthways and widthways. Mark these folds with a line of tacking (basting) stitches if desired. Start stitching from the centre of the Musical Pillow chart on page 20. Work the stitches over two threads of the fabric using two strands of cotton (floss) for the cross stitch and one strand for the backstitch, except for the lettering which should be in two strands.

2 When you have completed all the stitching, press your work face down on a soft cloth (see page 126). With the right side of the stitched piece facing you, pin the gathered edge of the lace around all the edges (keeping the lace pointing down towards the centre of the work). Tack (baste) or machine stitch the lace to the fabric at this stage.

3 Cut the hanging ribbon to the desired length, fold it in half and position on your fabric 1in (2.5cm) away from the edge, keeping the ends even. The loop will be inside the work so pin this down to keep it in position.

4 Find the centre of the backing fabric and with sharp scissors, cut a small hole for the music box key. Finish off neatly with buttonhole stitch in a matching colour.

5 Put the backing and front pieces together with right sides touching. Sew a ¼in (6mm) seam round the edges leaving an opening at the bottom large enough for you to insert the music box.

6 Clip the corners and turn the right way out, press, and stuff with some of the filling and the music box. Attach a small piece of double-sided tape to the case of the music box to attach it to the filling and prevent it from moving around too much when being wound. Carefully push the shank through the hole in the seam and screw in the key. Stuff the pillow until it is fairly firm, then slip stitch the opening. Attach the mother-of-pearl buttons to the ends of the hanging ribbon.

SAFETY NOTE

THE TINY BUTTONS ON THIS MUSICAL PILLOW MAKE IT UNSUITABLE AS A TOY FOR A BABY.

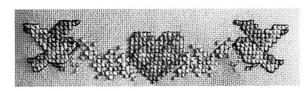

MUSICAL PILLOW

DMC

Cross stitch

⊡ 01	White	
◀ 334	Baby Blue - med	
⊠ 356	Terra Cotta - med	
T 368	Pistachio Green - lt	
● 433	Brown Golden - med	
━ 435	Brown Golden - v lt	
J 437	Tan - lt	
✳ 519	Sky Blue	
⊿ 648	Beaver Grey - dk	
⊟ 676	Golden Sand - lt	

Y 677	Golden Sand - v lt	
I 680	Golden Sand - dk	
◖ 726	Topaz - lt	
◣ 729	Golden Sand - med	
◥ 739	Tan - ultra v lt	
⧄ 747	Sky Blue - v lt	
☐ 754	Peach - lt	
4 758	Terra Cotta - v lt	
⧄ 761	Salmon - lt	
⊡ 775	Baby Blue - v lt	

☐ 950	Desert Sand - lt	
⧄ 3072	Beaver Grey - v lt	
∩ 3340	Apricot - med	
7 3341	Apricot	
⊞ 3756	Baby Blue - ultra v lt	
⊟ 3770	Tawny - v lt	
▶ 3773	Desert Sand - med	
⊟ 3774	Desert Sand - v lt	
← 3823	Yellow - ultra pale	
⋀ 3824	Apricot - lt	

Backstitch

━ 320	Pistachio Green - med
━ 356	Terra Cotta - med
━ 433	Brown Golden - med
━ 646	Beaver Grey - dk
━ 680	Golden Sand - dk
━ 838	Beige Brown - v dk
┅ 840	Beige Brown - med
━ 3772	Desert Sand - v dk

French knot

● 838	Beige Brown - v dk

STITCH NOTES

Worked over two on 28-count evenweave using two strands for cross stitch. Lettering in two strands; other backstitch in one strand.

Cherub Mobile

Mischievous cherubs float on golden wings on this mobile for the cot. Tiny star charms catch the light as it moves. I constructed my mobile from a special plastic ring with holes for strings that you can buy from craft shops. You could also use a flexi-hoop for the base.

◆

YOU WILL NEED

* Cream 14-count aida, 4 x 4in (10 x 10cm) for each cherub
* DMC stranded cotton (floss) as listed in the key
* White ¼in (5mm) double-faced satin ribbon, 2¼yds (2m)
* ⅝in (15mm) ribbon, cream with gold edging, 1¼yds (1.15m)
* Six white ready-made ribbon bows, roses or similar
* White felt with adhesive backing
* Eighteen small gold star charms
* Gold fabric angel wings, 2⅜ x 1⅜in (6 x 3.5cm), 6 pairs (optional, see below)
* Purpose-made plastic ring with holes, 6⅜in (16cm) diameter
* Needlework finisher
* Clear glue

1 Stitch the Cherub chart below in the centre of six pieces of cream aida, using two strands for the cross stitch and one strand for the backstitch Choose colourway 1 for girls, colourway 2 for boys, or alternate between the two. If you are using the fabric wings, do not stitch the wings on your design.

2 When you have completed all six cherubs, apply some needlework finisher to each one to stiffen it.

Leave to dry before adding the felt backing. Many craft shops sell felt with an adhesive backing which gives an excellent finish and is easy to use.

3 Carefully cut out round each cherub and stitch three tiny gold star charms to the bottom edge of each cloud.

4 Use the narrow ribbon to hang the cherubs from the mobile. They look better if they hang at different levels, so decide exactly how you want the finished project to look before cutting the ribbon and gluing it on to the back of each cherub.

5 Using a small dab of glue, attach the fabric wings (if used) to each cherub's back.

6 Space the cherubs out evenly around the ring and attach with the ribbons. Finish off by gluing on the tiny ribbon bows or roses.

7 Divide the cream ribbon into three equal lengths and attach it to the ring. Adjust as necessary to ensure the mobile will hang level and secure.

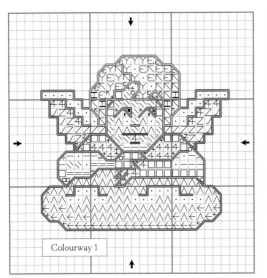

Colourway 1

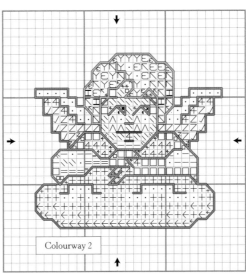

Colourway 2

CHERUBS ON A CLOUD

DMC

Cross stitch

·⌐·	01	⟋⟋	3072
◀◀	334	✚✚	3756
●●	433	⊟⊟	3770
⟋⟋	648	⊟⊟	3774
⊒⊒	676	◄◄	3823
⅄⅄	677		
⊥⊥	680	**Backstitch**	
◥◥	729	——	356
◣◣	739	——	646
☐☐	754	——	680
4⃞4⃞	758	——	840
⟋⟋	761	——	3772

Cherubs and Charms Keepsakes

Cherubs sit amid a froth of lace, ribbons and gold charms on heart-shaped keepsakes which would make a perfect greeting to give to a new mother (or grandma!) as an alternative to a conventional card.

◆

Lacy Heart Keepsake

YOU WILL NEED

- Two cherubs stitched and finished following the same method as for the mobile
- Heart-shaped wire frame with opening for threading lace, 6¾ x 6¼in (17 x 16cm)
- Cream 2½in (6.5cm) double-sided lace with centre perforation for threading on to the frame, 2¼yds (2m)
- Antique gold 1in (2.5cm) wire-edged ribbon, 11¾in (30cm)
- Cream ⅝in (15mm) ribbon with gold edging, 18in (46cm)
- Assorted gold charms, angels, hearts, stars, etc.

1 Thread the lace on to the wire frame and arrange evenly. Securely glue the cherubs to the lace.

2 Make the cream ribbon into a hanging loop, attach this to the centre of the heart and finish off with a charm.

3 Tie the wire-edged ribbon in a bow. Secure the centre with matching thread, neaten the ends and glue at the base of the heart.

4 Scatter charms around the lace and secure them with a few stitches.

◆

Small Heart Keepsake

YOU WILL NEED

- Cream 28-count jobelan, 4 x 4in (10 x 10cm)
- DMC stranded cotton (floss) as listed in the key
- Medium-sized heart-shaped hanger*
- Gold heart charms, one large and two small
- Three ribbon roses
- Ribbon and pearl rosette
- ⅜in (8mm) double-faced satin ribbon, 18in (46cm)
- Clear glue

1 Find the centre of the jobelan by folding it in half lengthways and widthways. Begin stitching the cherub chart on page 21 from the centre, working over two threads of the fabric and using two strands for the cross stitch and one strand for the backstitch.

2 Press your work (see page 126) and secure it in the heart shape following the instructions provided.

3 Add one large, and two small heart charms to the bottom of the frame, securing with a few stitches.

4 Thread the ribbon through the heart hanger and secure in a loop. Trim with ribbon roses and a rosette.

NOTE

*These metal shapes have a separate back so you can secure your stitched fabric without gluing and a locket-style hanger.

Angel Afghan

What could make a better heirloom project then a cosy afghan with angels standing guard in each corner to go on baby's cot? Use any combination of motifs to create your own unique gift.

◆

YOU WILL NEED

- Zweigart Anne afghan fabric, 28 x 45in (72 x 115cm)
- DMC stranded cotton (floss) as listed in the key
- White fleecy fabric or similar for backing, 23 x 40in (58.4 x 103cm) (optional)

1 I decorated my afghan with the angels from the bottom corners of the birth sampler chart on pages 16–17 and the verse charted on page 24. Stitch the motifs over two threads of the fabric using all six strands for the cross stitch and three strands for the backstitch. Count two stitches for every one shown on the sampler chart to make the angels the large size shown in the photograph. To help with placement, cut a piece of paper to the finished size and pin onto the fabric. Tack (baste) around the edge of this, remove the paper and begin stitching.

2 Find the centre of the middle panel of the afghan and stitch the verse on page 24 starting in the centre. Stitch a tiny heart in each intersection of the woven grid around the outside of the afghan as shown if using Anne cloth.

3 Add a fleecy backing to make the afghan more cosy and improve the look of the finished project. Turn under the edges of the fleecy fabric ¼in (6mm) and press. It is important to wash and press the stitched afghan at this stage (see page 126). Pin the backing to the afghan with wrong sides together and using the woven afghan grid as a guideline. When you are happy with the position, slip stitch the backing in place.

4 Make a fringe for the afghan by pulling out the horizontal threads one by one on each side as far as the start of the stitched design.

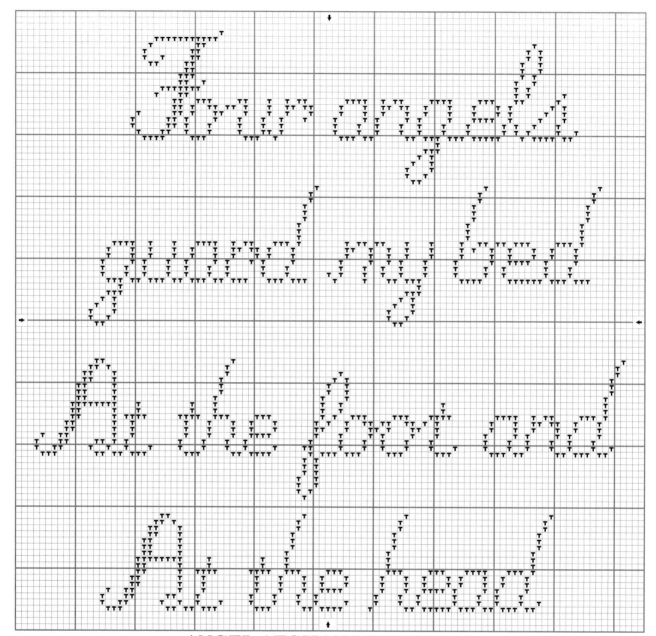

ANGEL AFGHAN LETTERING

DMC

Cross stitch

T T 931 Antique Blue - med

STITCH NOTES

Stitched over two threads on Anne afghan fabric using six strands for cross stitch and three strands for backstitch.
Verse chart for centre panel shown above. Four angels taken from the bottom corners of the birth sampler on page 17: count two stitches for every one shown on the chart to make the finished size of each angel 64w by 88h.

DMC stranded cottons have been used throughout. The thread requirements for this project are as follows: White (13 skeins), 646 (2 skeins), 648 (3 skeins), 775 (3 skeins), 950 (4 skeins), 3756 (3 skeins), 3774 (5 skeins), 3823 (5 skeins). For all other colours, both cross stitch and backstitch, one skein is required.

Hands to Work – Hearts to God

At times we wish we could swap our hectic lives for a simpler way of living, one measured by the rhythm of the seasons rather than by the hands of a clock. But how many of us would be willing to exchange the comforts of modern living for the rigorous life of the hardworking Amish people? Surrounded only by the bare necessities, they rise at dawn to spend long days cultivating the land. But for them the rewards of such labour are clear: 'Hands to Work – Hearts to God.'

Whether you spend your time gardening, or as I am privileged to do, drawing and designing, being creative is good for the soul. I have portrayed the simple traditions of the Amish way of life in these gardening designs. There's a herb-filled cushion, a sturdy apron, a basket for filling with gifts, and a willow wreath to remind us that we really do reap what we sow.

◆

This charming Amish design uses only whole cross stitch and backstitch and is straightforward to complete. It would also look good mounted in a simple wooden frame to hang on a kitchen wall. And why not make a different cushion, this time using the motifs from the willow wreath?

Willow Wreath

Give a special country look to these heartfelt words by framing them in a tiny willow heart trimmed with a ribbon bow and a charm.

◆

DESIGN SIZE: 3⅜ x 2½in (8.5 x 6.5cm)
STITCH COUNT: 47 wide x 35 high

◆

YOU WILL NEED

* Sand 28-count evenweave, 7 x 7in (17.5 x 17.5cm)
* DMC stranded cotton (floss) as listed in the key
* Tapestry needle, size 26
* Woven willow heart (see page 127)
(these are often handmade so check the aperture is large enough to hold the design)
* Stiff card or mount board, the size of the willow heart
* Craft knife
* Clear glue
* Felt for backing
* Double-sided tape
* Wire-edged ribbon, 12in (30.5cm)
* Pewter farmyard charm (barn shown)

1 Find the centre of your fabric by folding it in half lengthways and widthways, and begin stitching from the centre of the chart below. Work the design over two threads of the fabric using two strands of cotton (floss)

for the cross stitch and one strand for the backstitch, and omitting the two red hearts. Refer to the key opposite.

2 Place the willow heart onto the piece of card and draw round it. Cut out this outline using a sharp craft knife. Place a piece of double-sided tape in the centre of the board to hold the stitched piece in position. Centre the cross stitch on the board and press down on the double-sided tape. Trim the excess fabric to about ½in (13mm) from the edge of the board. Carefully fold and stick the fabric to the back of the board. Cover the back with a piece of felt to neaten.

3 Using clear glue, stick the mounted piece to the back of the willow heart. It will probably be quite uneven so you may need to hold the woven heart and the stitched piece together until they are secured. Tie a bow in the wire-edged ribbon and stitch a pewter charm to the centre. Stick this neatly in place at the bottom of the wreath with glue or a few stitches.

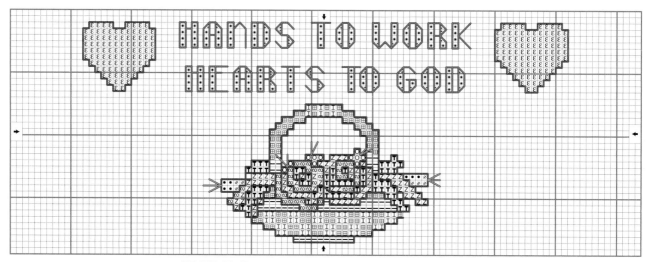

WILLOW WREATH/BASKET

HANDS TO WORK HEARTS TO GOD

DMC
Cross stitch

01	White	433	Brown Golden - med
310	Black	435	Brown Golden - v lt
211	Lavender - lt	437	Tan - lt
318	Silver Grey - lt	452	Shell Grey - med
319	Pistachio Green - v dk	453	Shell Grey - lt
320	Pistachio Green - med	676	Golden Sand - lt
368	Pistachio Green - lt	722	Orange Spice - lt
415	Silver Grey	729	Golden Sand - med

797	Royal Blue	3779	Terracotta - ultra v lt
798	Delft Blue - dk	3782	Mocha Brown - lt
799	Delft Blue - med	3820	Straw - dk
800	Delft Blue - pale	3823	Yellow - ultra pale
945	Tawny		
951	Tawny - lt	**Backstitch**	
993	Aquamarine - lt	320	Pistachio - med
3328	Salmon - dk	792	Cornflower Blue - dk
		838	Beige Brown - v dk

STITCH NOTES

Stitched over two threads on 28-count evenweave using two strands for cross stitch throughout. Backstitch in one strand.

Apron

Stitched on rustico aida fabric without the border on the main chart, the picture of the Amish couple make the perfect finishing touch for a green cotton gardening apron.

◆

DESIGN SIZE: 5¾ x 5¾in (14.5 x 14.5cm)
STITCH COUNT: 80 wide x 79 high

◆

YOU WILL NEED

* 14-count Rustico aida, 8½ x 8½in (22 x 22cm)
* DMC stranded cotton (floss) as listed in the key
* Matching sewing cotton
* Tapestry needle, size 24
* Gardening apron

1 Find the centre of the aida fabric by folding it in half lengthways and widthways. Mark these folds with tacking (basting) stitches if desired. Stitch the Amish couple and the lettering from the chart on page 29, but omit the patchwork border and make the bottom edge finish below the carrots. You will probably find it useful to make a photocopy of the chart and mark the borders of this new chart and its centre point on it, and then stitch from this new version. Refer to the photograph if you need to. Then begin stitching from the centre, using two strands of cotton (floss) for the cross stitch and one strand for the backstitch.

2 Turn under and press a ½in (13mm) hem all round your completed stitching. Pin in position on the front of the gardening apron and neatly stitch in place.

Gift Basket

Decorated with part of the Amish design set on a crisp gingham background and embellished with gold charms, this willow basket is just right for filling with gardening gifts or a potted plant.

◆

DESIGN SIZE: 5¾ x 2½in (14.5 x 6.5cm)
STITCH COUNT: 80 wide x 35 high

◆

YOU WILL NEED

* Sand 28-count evenweave, 8 x 5in (20.5 x 12.5cm)
* Gingham fabric, 8½ x 26in (21.5 x 66cm)
* DMC stranded cotton (floss) as listed in the key
* Tapestry needle, size 26
* Four gold gardening charms or decorative buttons
* Matching sewing cotton
* Woven willow basket with handle, 8in (20cm) diameter
* Round elastic, 20in (½m)
* Wire-edged checked ribbon, 18in (46cm)
* Darning needle

1 Find the centre of your fabric by folding it in half lengthways and widthways. Find the centre of the chart on page 28 and begin stitching from here. Work the design over two threads of the fabric using two strands of cotton (floss) for the cross stitch and one strand for the backstitch outlining. Refer to the key on page 29.

2 When you have completed all the stitching, securely attach the gardening charms or buttons using matching sewing cotton. Refer to the photograph on page 26 for placement. Turn under and press the raw edges of your work ½in (13mm) to the wrong side.

3 Cut the gingham, adjusting the measurements if you have a different-size basket. With wrong sides facing, put the long edges together and sew a ¼in (6mm) seam. Turn the right way out and press. On the right side, sew two further lines of stitches, one ¼in (6mm) away from the seam and one ¼in (6mm) away from the top to make the channels for the elastic.

4 Sew the design in the centre of the gingham, keeping the seam at the bottom. Using a darning needle, thread elastic through the channels at the top and bottom and secure it at one end. Fit the band around the basket and join with neat slip stitches. Tighten the elastic to fit and secure. Trim the handle of your basket with a bow made from wire-edged ribbon. Fill as desired.

Herb Pillow

Trimmed with antique buttons and set against a simple cotton fabric background, this herb pillow design of an Amish farmer and his wife holding a basket of produce fresh from their garden, would make a charming gift for a gardening enthusiast.

◆

DESIGN SIZE: 7⅛ x 7⅛in (18 x 18cm)
STITCH COUNT: 100 wide x 100 high

◆

YOU WILL NEED

* Blue grey 28-count evenweave, 14 x 14in (35.5 x 35.5cm)
* Cotton fabric, 45in (115cm) wide, 39in (1m)
* DMC stranded cotton (floss) as listed in the key
* Tapestry needle, size 26
* Four buttons (old ones are the nicest)
* Cushion pad, 16in (40.5cm)
* Sachet of herbs or lavender (optional)

1 Find the centre of the fabric by folding it in half lengthways and widthways. Mark the folds with a line of tacking (basting) stitches if desired. Stitch the 'Hands to Work – Hearts to God' chart on page 29, starting in the centre. Work the design over two threads of the fabric, using two strands of cotton (floss) for the cross stitch and one strand for the backstitch.

2 When the stitching is complete, trim the evenweave so that it measures 12 x 12in (30.5 x 30.5cm). Turn under and press ½in (13mm) all round.

3 Cut a 19 x 19in (48 x 48cm) piece of cotton fabric for the front of the cushion. Place the wrong side of the stitched piece in the centre of the right side of the cushion front, leaving a 4in (10cm) border of fabric showing all round. Tack and sew the stitched piece in place. Sew a button in each corner.

4 Cut a piece of cotton fabric for the back of the cushion measuring 19in (48cm) wide but 24in (61cm) long. Cut this in half widthways. Turn under a ⅝in (15mm) hem to the wrong side down one long edge of each piece and stitch.

5 Lay the front on top of the backing pieces, with right sides together and the hemmed edges of the backing pieces overlapping. Pin, tack (baste) and sew a ⅝in (15mm) seam all round. Trim the seams and clip the corners, then turn the cushion cover to the right side and press (see page 126).

6 To give a simple but stylish look to the cushion, measure in 2in (5cm) all round from the edges. Mark with a line of tacking (basting) stitches. On the right side of the cushion follow this line and sew through all layers with a straight machine stitch. To give a more decorative finish, a zig-zag or satin stitch can be used. Insert the cushion pad and small sachet of scented herbs or lavender if desired.

The Lord's Prayer

One of my earliest memories of the little Church-in-Wales primary school I attended is of learning the Lord's Prayer and reciting it to our teachers. One of these was Miss Beech, who helped me with many of the quotations that inspired the designs in this book. We never forget good teachers and Miss Beech was certainly one of those. She encouraged a love of reading and writing which has never left me. So I decided to use an image from childhood to illustrate this most familiar prayer. The young shepherd and his faithful dog tend their flock on a sunlit hillside, watched over by a guiding but unseen presence. Just as we are protected and nurtured by those that shape our young lives. Parents, grandparents, teachers, all help to bring us to fruitful adulthood so we can pass our experiences on to the next generation. This project is for everyone who had a Miss Beech in their lives to guide and inspire them, and for whom the simple beliefs of childhood have stood the test of time.

◆

DESIGN SIZE: 7⅜ x 10⅜in (18.5 x 26.5cm)
STITCH COUNT: 103 wide x 146 high

◆

YOU WILL NEED
* Antique white 14-count aida, 14 x 17in (35.5 x 43cm)
* DMC stranded cotton (floss) as listed in the key
* Tapestry needle, size 24
* Mount board, 12 x 15in (30.5 x 38cm)
* Picture frame of your choice

1 Find the centre of the fabric by folding it in half lengthways and widthways. Mark this with a line of tacking (basting) stitches if desired. Starting from the centre, stitch the design from the chart on pages 34–35, using two strands of cotton (floss) for the cross stitch and one strand for the backstitch including all the lettering. Work the French knots in one strand.

2 Parts of the chart are worked in half cross stitch to give depth to the design – the clouds and the hills in the background. These are listed separately in the key with the number of strands to use indicated in brackets.

3 When you have completed all the stitching, press your work and prepare it for framing (see page 126). A professional framer will be able to cut a shaped mount like the one shown in the photograph.

◆

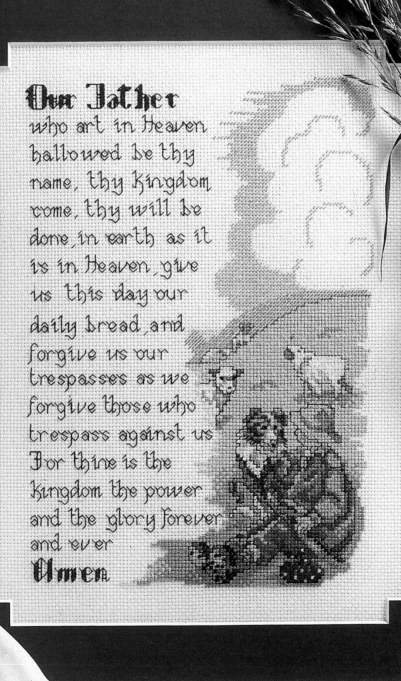

Our Father
who art in Heaven
hallowed be thy
name, thy kingdom
come, thy will be
done, in earth as it
is in Heaven, give
us this day our
daily bread, and
forgive us our
trespasses as we
forgive those who
trespass against us
For thine is the
kingdom the power
and the glory forever
and ever
Amen.

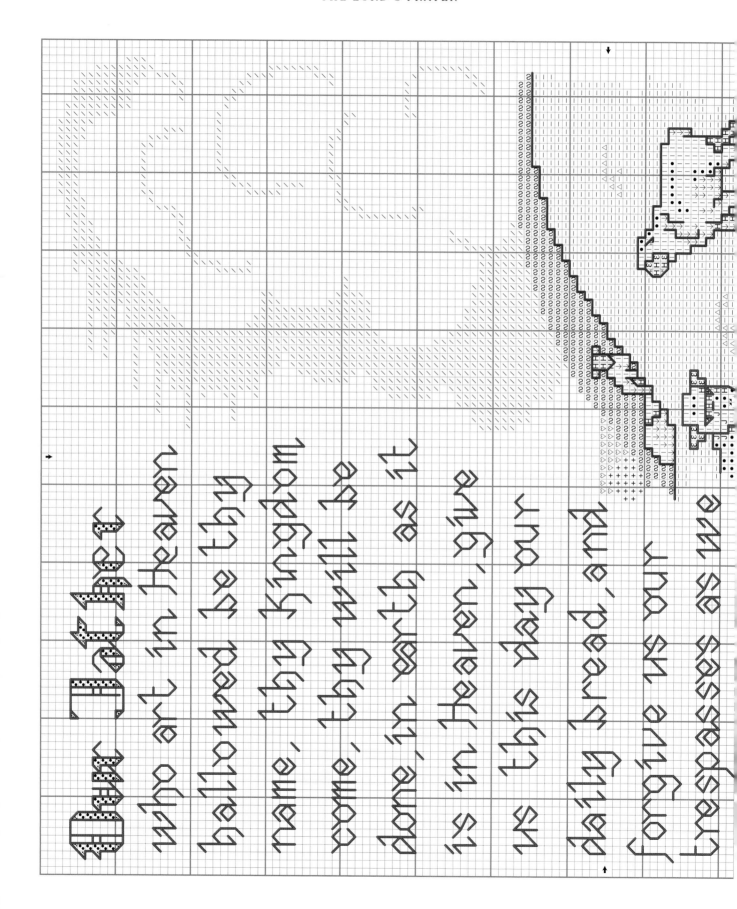

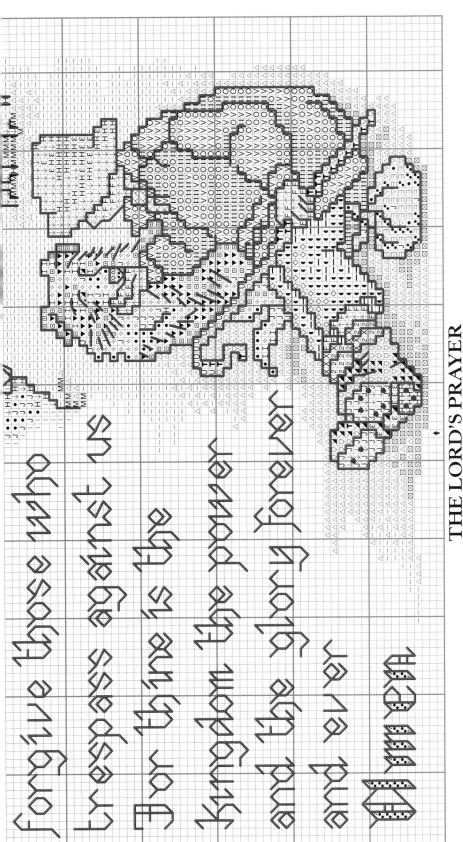

THE LORD'S PRAYER

DMC

Cross stitch

·	01	White
V V	341	Blue Violet - lt
▷	351	Peach
⊠	370	Mustard - med
M M	371	Mustard
△	372	Mustard - lt
▶	433	Brown Golden - med
□	435	Brown Golden - v lt
I I	437	Tan - lt
- -	472	Avocado Green - ultra lt
••	498	Christmas Red - dk
ε ε	640	Beige Grey - v dk
H H	642	Beige Grey - dk
↓ ↓	644	Beige Grey - med

I I	712	Cream
V	739	Tan - ultra v lt
K	742	Tangerine - lt
K	744	Yellow - pale
F F	758	Terracotta - v lt
H H	792	Cornflower Blue - dk
O O	793	Cornflower Blue - med
⊟	817	Coral Red - v dk
✗	838	Beige Brown - v dk
T T	839	Beige Brown - dk
U U	840	Beige Brown - med
2 2	841	Beige Brown - lt
X X	931	Antique Blue - med
	932	Antique Blue - lt

↑ ↑	945	Tawny
-	975	Rust - v dk
J J	3023	Brown Grey - lt
●●	3799	Pewter Grey - v dk
◀	3826	Rust - dk
◇◇	3827	Rust - v lt

Half cross stitch

▽▽	453	Shell Grey - med (1)
++	451	Shell Grey - dk (1)
//	341	Blue Violet - lt (1)
◎◎	452	Shell Grey - med (1)

Backstitch

—— 838 Beige Brown - v dk
—— 3790 Beige Grey - ultra dk

French knots

● 838 Beige Brown - v dk

STITCH NOTES

Stitched on 14-count aida using two strands for cross stitch. Half cross stitch in the number of strands indicated in brackets. Backstitch and French knots in one strand.

Summer
LIFE'S BOUNTY

Just as a garden blossoms into beauty in the summer sun, so our lives begin their most bountiful years as we enter adulthood. This is the time when we lay the foundations for our own futures and for those of our growing families.

In this section we begin with a glimpse of a glorious summer day on the second of the seasonal banners. In fact, it's the kind of day that's perfect for a wedding celebration, and you'll find a whole series of designs to mark such an important milestone in our lives. There's an elegant sampler for recording the names of the happy couple, and many other gifts to give as keepsakes on such a special occasion. Trimmed with lace, charms and beads, they will make charming mementos to treasure. Friendship is another of life's riches, and this is celebrated in a picture of a young boy and his faithful dog.

Summer is a wonderful time of year for gardeners as they sit back to enjoy the fruits of their labour. The lovely cushion and other pretty gifts based on a knot garden are meant for them. For many of us, summer holds memories of holidays by the sea, so it seemed appropriate to include a stunning silhouette of a lighthouse. As well as being a beautiful subject in its own right, it serves to remind us that from time to time we all look for a light in the darkness to guide us to a safe harbour.

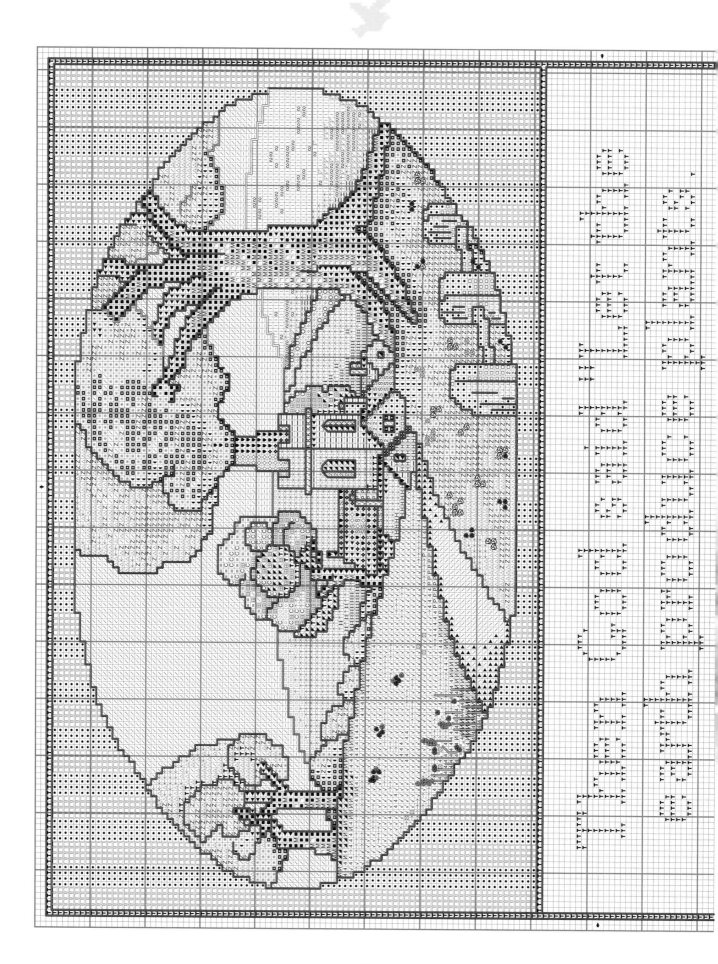

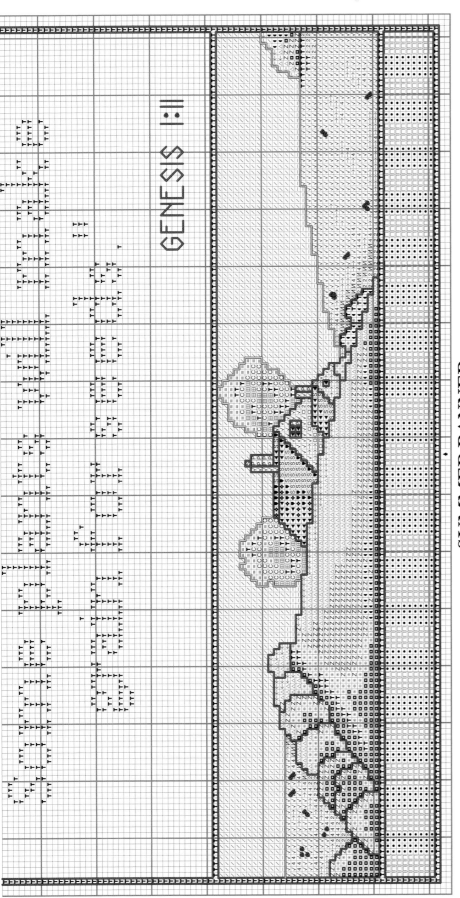

GENESIS 1:11

SUMMER BANNER

DMC

Cross stitch

·	01	White	
❖	300	Mahogany - v dk	
◆	301	Mahogany - med	
⊠	321	Christmas Red	
◇	402	Mahogany - v lt	
◉	469	Avocado Green	
Z	470	Avocado Green - lt	
△	471	Avocado Green - v lt	
←	472	Avocado Green - ultra lt	
K	520	Fern Green - dk	
⊞	522	Fern Green	
C	523	Fern Green - lt	
=	524	Fern Green - v lt	

—	640	Beige Grey - v dk
H	642	Beige Grey - dk
↓	644	Beige Grey - med
▲	647	Beaver Grey - med
\	648	Beaver Grey - lt
→	676	Golden Sand - lt
V	677	Golden Sand - v lt
И	680	Golden Sand - dk
4	729	Golden Sand - med
□	741	Tangerine - med
▼	839	Beige Brown - dk
■	840	Beige Brown - med
M	841	Beige Brown - lt
⊤	842	Beige Brown - v lt

T	931	Antique Blue - med
⊡	936	Avocado Green - dk
◀	937	Avocado Green - med
÷	3022	Brown Grey - med
K	3023	Brown Grey - lt
2	3041	Silver Plum - med
□	3042	Silver Plum - lt
V	3045	Yellow Beige - lt
P	3045	Yellow Beige - dk
⊥	3743	Silver Plum - lt
S	3776	Mahogany - lt
▨	3787	Brown Grey - dk

Half cross stitch

O	647	Beaver Grey - med
⊠	676	Golden Sand - lt

⫿	677	Golden Sand - v lt
⊞	680	Golden Sand - dk
⧄	729	Golden Sand - med
—	775	Baby Blue - v lt
H	3041	Silver Plum - med
⬆	3042	Silver Plum - lt
⬚	3072	Beaver Grey - v lt
◎	3743	Silver Plum - med
⧄	3755	Baby Blue - v lt

Long stitch

—	676	Golden Sand - lt
—	838	Beige Brown - v dk

—	469	Avocado Green (2)
—	680	Golden Sand - dk (2)

French knots

⊕	01	White
•	321	Christmas Red
⊛	470	Avocado Green - lt
⊛	680	Golden Sand - dk
⊛	743	Yellow - med
•	839	Beige Brown - dk
•	3731	Dusty Rose - v dk

Backstitch

—	931	Antique Blue - med
—	938	Coffee Brown - ultra v dk
—	3042	Silver Plum - lt
—	647	Beaver Grey - med

STITCH NOTES

Stitched on 14-count aida using two strands for cross stitch and half cross stitch. Backstitch and French knots in one strand. Long stitch in two strands. DMC stranded cottons used throughout. One skein of each colour is required to complete the design except for white and 741 (2 skeins).

Summer Hanging Banner

It is now noon on a perfect summer's day in the valley. The old tree in the foreground beckons us into the picture with the welcoming shade of its dense foliage. At its roots, a carpet of lush grass starred with tiny wildflowers seems the perfect place to spread a cloth and enjoy a leisurely picnic.
On either side of the winding road, fields of golden corn studded with glowing red poppies ripen in the brilliant sunshine. The trees and hedgerows are dappled with blue shadows and the distant hills recede in a shimmer of heat haze to the arch of a cloudless sky. What lies over the hill? You can decide that as you stitch, but I like to think it is a vista of sparkling blue water fringing a great sweep of sandy bay. Just like the first glimpse of the sea remembered from childhood holidays.

◆

DESIGN SIZE: 10¾ x 14½in (27.5 x 37cm)
STITCH COUNT: 151 wide x 205 high

◆

YOU WILL NEED

* Cream 14-count aida, 15 x 18in (38 x 46cm)
* White cotton backing fabric, 20in (50cm)
* DMC stranded cotton (floss) as listed in the key
* Tapestry needle, size 24
* Silk cord, 2¼yds (2m)
* Large wooden bell-pull or doweling and wooden knobs for hanging

1 Find the centre of your fabric by folding it in half lengthways and widthways. Mark this with two lines of tacking (basting) stitches if desired. Starting from the middle, stitch the Summer Banner from the chart on pages 38–39, using two strands of cotton (floss) for the cross stitch and one strand for the backstitch. Some areas of this design are stitched in half cross stitch to give the effect of a receding background. These are also worked in two strands and listed separately in the key.

2 Follow the key carefully when working the backstitch because several different colours are used to give the project depth. The poppy stems and cornstalks in the left foreground are sewn as long stitches using two strands of 469 and 680 respectively. Work the French knots in one strand.

3 When you have completed all the stitching, press your work (see page 126) and turn to page 14 for directions on how to make up the banner.

With This Ring I Thee Wed

'So let us love, dear love, like as we ought,
love is the lesson which the Lord us taught.'

EDMUND SPENSER

*T*hese lines seemed perfect to go on a sampler that celebrates such an important occasion as a wedding. I decided they lent themselves to an elegant Regency-style design complete with gilded scrolls, ribbons, and cartouches for displaying the couple's initials. The same Regency theme is continued in the collection of wedding gifts, to which I gave an heirloom look by using delicate colours and adding lavish trimmings. As well as the wedding sampler, you can also make two traditional symbols of good luck – an elegant wedding slipper stitched on perforated paper and a beautiful lacy horseshoe decorated with a pretty white dove. A ring pillow depicts the clasped hands of the happy couple within the same border that appears on the sampler. You can also stitch elements of the design to decorate a tiny bag for holding confetti, a keepsake box and a handsome box frame to fill with reminders of this special day.

◆

The Wedding Sampler

DESIGN SIZE: 7¾ x 10¾in (19.5 x 27.5cm)
STITCH COUNT: 109 wide x 150 high

◆

YOU WILL NEED

- Antique white 28-count evenweave, 14 x 17in (35.5 x 43cm)
- DMC stranded cotton (floss) as listed in the key
- Kreinik Blending Filament, Shade 002, gold
- Tapestry needle, size 26
- Beading needle (optional)
- DMC seed beads, V3.08.3046, Pale gold
- Graph paper and pencil
- Mount board, 12 x 15in (30.5 x 38cm)
- Picture frame of your choice

1 Find the centre of your fabric by folding it in half lengthways and widthways and marking these folds with a line of tacking (basting) stitches if desired. Find the centre of the Wedding Sampler chart on pages 44–45 and start by stitching the central rose and ribbon scroll.

TIP

*W*HY NOT CHANGE THE COLOUR OF THE STITCHED RIBBONS ON THESE PROJECTS TO MATCH YOUR BRIDE'S COLOUR SCHEME. I USED SIX SHADES OF BLUE PLUS WHITE ON THESE RIBBONS TO CREATE THE EFFECT OF SATIN, BUT YOU CAN EASILY SUBSTITUTE, SAY, PINKS FOR THE BLUES ON THIS CHART. VISIT YOUR LOCAL NEEDLEWORK SHOP WHERE YOU WILL HAVE ALL THE COTTON COLOURS TO HAND. FIND A GOOD RANGE OF SHADES FROM LIGHT TO DARK TO GET THE SAME EFFECT ON YOUR RIBBON. CHANGE THE COLOURS OF THE ROSES, TOO, OR SUBSTITUTE THEM WITH BEADS FOR A VERY SPECIAL SAMPLER.

So let us Love dear
love, like as we
ought
Love is the lesson
which the Lord
is taught

S   A

SUE
and
ADRIAN

28th May 1982

You will find it helpful for positioning the letters if you stitch this motif first.

2 Use two strands of cotton (floss) for the cross stitch and half cross stitch, and one strand for the backstitch, including the lettering. Where blending filament is required, thread the needle with two strands of cotton (floss) and one strand of the filament.

3 Draw out the names of your couple and the wedding date on graph paper using the alphabets on page 47. Use the sampler chart as a guide for spacing the letters. When you are happy with the way they look, stitch them on your sampler, counting down the same number of stitches from the central rose and ribbon scroll. Draw out the oval shape for the initials on your graph paper and chart the couple's initials using the upper-case alphabet, and positioning them centrally in the oval. When you are happy with the way they look stitch them on your sampler.

4 Attach a bead for each symbol on the chart using one strand of matching cotton and securing each one with a half cross stitch (see page 125).

5 When you have completed all the stitching, press your work and prepare it for framing (see page 126).

The Ring Pillow

Clasped hands symbolise the happy couple within a border in the same style as the sampler. Wedding rings and an ornate heart charm have been used as well as a three-dimensional little golden heart on the bride's bracelet.

◆

DESIGN SIZE: 7¾ x 6¼in (19.5 x 17cm)
STITCH COUNT: 109 wide x 95 high

◆

YOU WILL NEED

- Antique white 28-count evenweave, 12 x 12in(30.5 x 30.5cm)
- Backing fabric, 10½ x 9½in (26.5 x 24cm)
- DMC stranded cotton (floss) as listed in the key
- Tapestry needle, size 26
- Beading needle
- DMC seed beads, V3.03.3046, Pale gold
- Wedding ring charms
- Ornate heart and 3-D golden heart charm (optional)
- Kreinik Fine Braid (8), shade 221, antique gold
- Insertion lace, 1½yds (1.25m)
- Filling, about 8oz

1 Find the centre of your fabric. Stitch the design from the Ring Pillow chart on page 46, starting in the centre. Work over two threads of the fabric using two strands of cotton (floss) for the cross stitch and half cross stitch. Use one strand for the backstitch and the French knots.

2 Attach a bead for each symbol on the chart using one strand of matching cotton and securing each one with a half cross stitch (see page 125).

3 Thread the wedding ring charms onto a loop of Kreinik No. 8 gold braid. Make sure this is long enough to allow the rings to hang from the bottom of the pillow before securing it with a few stitches at the back. Add the other heart charms if desired.

4 To make up the pillow, trim the stitched piece to the same size as the piece of backing fabric.

5 With right sides together, join the stitched front and the backing piece by sewing a ¼in (6mm) seam round the edges. Leave an opening in the bottom edge large enough to add the filling. Clip the corners, and turn the pillow the right way out. Attach the lace around the edges of the pillow. Insert the filling, fold under the open edges and slip stitch them neatly together.

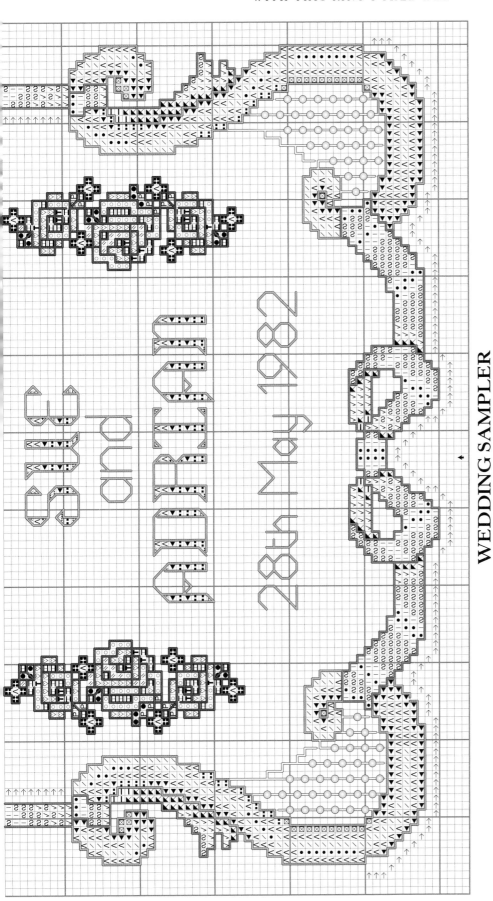

WEDDING SAMPLER

DMC

Cross stitch

· ·	01	White
— —	312	Baby Blue - v dk
P P	320	Pistachio Green - med
◤◤	322	Baby Blue - dk
√ √	334	Baby Blue - med
T T	350	Peach - med
Ⅱ Ⅱ	351	Peach
▽ ▽	352	Peach - lt
○ ○	353	Peach - v lt
● ●	367	Pistachio Green - dk
S S	452	Shell Grey - med
+ +	453	Shell Grey - lt
∧ ∧	725	Topaz
∕ ∕	727	Topaz - v lt +
		Kreinik 002 Gold
		blending filament (1)
– –	746	Off White
‖ ‖	775	Baby Blue - v lt
⊠ ⊠	781	Topaz - v dk
⦙ ⦙	782	Topaz - dk
▼ ▼	783	Topaz - med
Y Y	800	Delft Blue - pale
▦ ▦	809	Delft Blue
⦚ ⦚	948	Peach - v lt
⊘ ⊘	3755	Baby Blue

Half cross stitch

→ →	452	Shell Grey - med

Backstitch

——	322	Baby Blue - dk
——	725	Topaz
——	780	Topaz - ultra v dk
——	838	Beige Brown - v dk

Beads

○		DMC seed beads,
		V3.08.3046 - pale gold

STITCH NOTES

Stitched over two on 28-count evenweave using two strands for cross stitch and half cross stitch. Combine with number of strands of blending filament indicated in brackets. Backstitch in one strand. Attach beads with half cross.

We give these rings as
a symbol of our Love

RING PILLOW

DMC

Cross stitch

·|·	01	White	Λ|Λ	725	Topaz
−|−	312	Baby Blue - v dk	∕|∕	727	Topaz - v lt +
P|P	320	Pistachio Green - med			Kreinik BF001, Gold
K|K	322	Baby Blue - dk	I|I	775	Baby Blue - v lt
√|√	334	Baby Blue - med	⊠|⊠	781	Topaz - v dk
T|T	350	Peach - med	•••|	782	Topaz - dk
I|I	351	Peach	◄|◄	783	Topaz - med
♡|♡	352	Peach - lt	⊗|⊗	945	Tawny
○|○	353	Peach - v lt	−|−	951	Tawny - lt
●|●	367	Pistachio Green - dk	∞|∞	3755	Baby Blue
S|S	452	Shell Grey - med			
+|+	453	Shell Grey - lt			

Half cross stitch

→|→	452	Shell Grey - med

Backstitch

⎯⎯⎯	322	Baby Blue - dk
⎯⎯⎯	725	Topaz
⎯⎯⎯	780	Topaz - ultra v dk
⎯⎯⎯	839	Beige Brown - v dk

Beads

○   DMC seed beads
    V3.03.3046 - pale gold

STITCH NOTES

Ring Pillow stitched over two threads on 28-count evenweave. Cross stitch and half cross stitch in two strands. Backstitch and French knots in one strand.

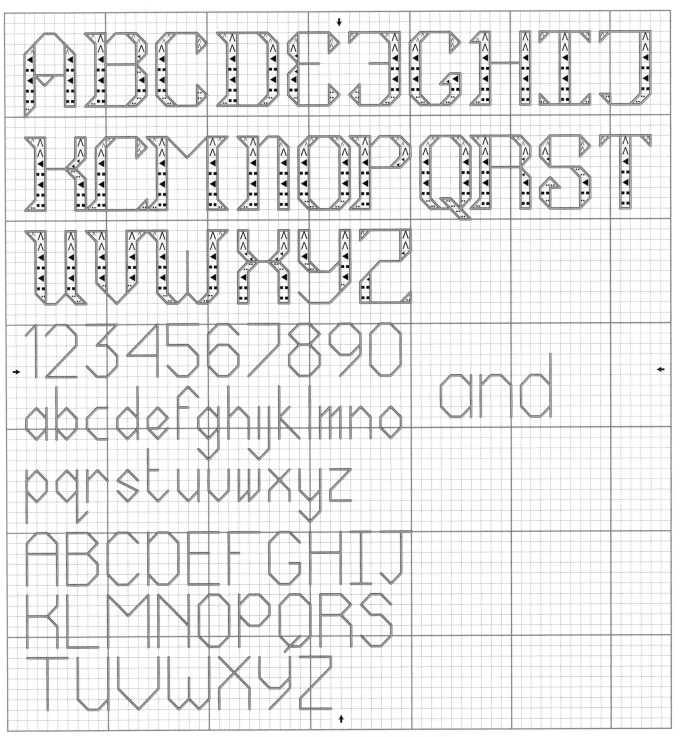

WEDDING ALPHABET

DMC

Cross stitch

∧ ∧	725	Topaz
•• ••	782	Topaz - dk
◀ ◀	783	Topaz - med

Backstitch

▬▬	780	Topaz - ultra v lt

Lacy Horseshoe

Make a traditional symbol of good luck decorated with a cross stitched dove for a bride. Trimmed with a covering of beautiful lace and a blue satin ribbon so the bride can carry it with her bouquet, this will be a lovely gift to treasure.

◆

DESIGN SIZE: 5 x 2½in (12.5 x 6.5cm)
STITCH COUNT : 69 wide x 34 high

◆

YOU WILL NEED

- Antique white 28-count evenweave, 6 x 4in (15 x 10cm)
- DMC stranded cotton (floss) as listed in the key
- Tapestry needle, size 26
- Needlework finisher or other fabric stiffener
- Scissors
- Paper or thin card for pattern
- Tracing paper
- Pencil
- Thick card or mount board, white, 8 x 10in (22 x 25.5cm)
- Craft knife
- Clear glue
- Wadding (batting), 8 x 10in (20.5 x 25.5cm)
- Cream Cluny lace with ribbon insert, 2in (5cm) wide, 78in (2m)
- String of cream pearl beads, 2¼yds (2m)
- Cream hearts trimming or similar for edging, 2¼yds (2m)
- Blue satin ribbon, 1½in (4cm) wide, 18in (46cm)
- Four pearl heart shapes or similar for trimming

1 Find the centre of your fabric by folding it in half lengthways and widthways. Stitch the dove design from the chart on page 50, starting in the centre.

2 Use two strands of cotton (floss) for the cross stitch and one strand for the backstitch.

3 When you have completed all the stitching, apply some needlework finisher to stiffen your work, following

Use these designs to make some beautiful wedding keepsakes.

the manufacturer's instructions. Put aside to dry before cutting round the shape of the dove close to the stitching.

4 Trace the outline of the horseshoe shape opposite and use this to cut a pattern from the paper or thin card. Draw around the pattern on the thick card or mount board and, using a sharp craft knife, cut out the horseshoe. White or cream mount board is best because it will not show through the lace and spoil the finished effect.

5 Cover one side of the cardboard horseshoe with a thin layer of clear glue and stick the wadding to it. Allow to dry before trimming the wadding (batting) to shape.

6 Neatly secure one edge of the Cluny lace to the top

right-hand side of the horseshoe by gluing or sticking with double-sided tape. With the wadding facing, begin to wrap the lace around the cardboard shape. Take your time and try to get a nice even covering. Do not wrap too tightly. The correct tension will give a smooth finish and make it unnecessary to stick the lace to the wadding. When you are happy with the effect, neatly secure the end of the lace at the back with a dab of glue.

7 Now decorate the shape with your chosen trimmings. Stitch your edging to the horseshoe, starting around the inside edge and continuing right round the whole shape before finishing off securely. Stitch or carefully glue the string of beads into place following the same method.

8 Referring to the photograph, stick the dove and the hearts or other trimmings to the lace with clear glue. Neatly secure a loop of satin ribbon to the top edges of the horseshoe with clear glue, checking that the finished piece will hang correctly when carried by the bride.

STITCH NOTES

Stitched over two threads on 28-count evenweave using two strands for cross stitch throughout. Backstitch in one strand.

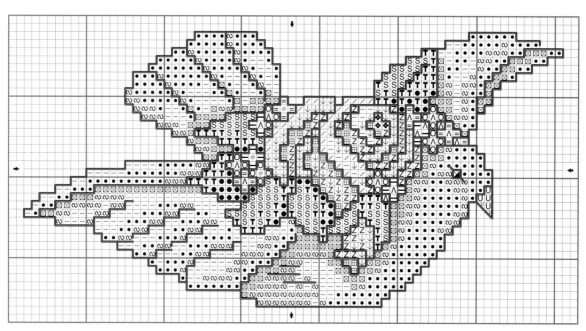

DOVE

DMC

Cross stitch

• 01 White	❖ 350 Peach - med	∞ 453 Shell Grey - lt	∕ 948 Peach - v lt
● 319 Pistachio Green - v dk	⊞ 351 Peach	∧ 725 Topaz	= 3755 Baby Blue - dk
S 320 Pistachio Green - med	Z 352 Peach - lt	⊘ 727 Topaz - v lt	
O 322 Baby Blue - dk	↓ 353 Peach - v lt	— 746 Off White	**Backstitch**
— 334 Baby Blue - med	T 367 Pistachio Green - dk	U 783 Topaz - v lt	— 838 Beige Brown - v dk
	⊠ 452 Shell Grey - med	◢ 838 Beige Brown - v dk	

ACTUAL SIZE TEMPLATE
SHOWING CUTTING
LINE FOR PERFORATED
PAPER AROUND
STITCHED SHOE DESIGN

ACTUAL SIZE TEMPLATE
FOR WEDDING HORSESHOE

𝔚edding 𝔖lipper

𝒮hoes are a favourite wedding keepsake so I designed a pretty slipper in the same Regency style as the sampler. Stitched on perforated paper, it is finished off with ribbon roses, beads, bows and a silk tassel.

◆

DESIGN SIZE: 7 x 3½in (17.5 x 8.5)
STITCH COUNT: 97 wide x 46 high

◆

YOU WILL NEED

* Cream or white 14-count perforated paper, 6 x 8in (15 x 20cm)
* DMC stranded cotton (floss) as listed in the key
* Anchor Marlitt thread, 1012, cream
* Kreinik Fine Braid No. 8 – 221, Antique gold
* Tapestry needle, size 24
* Beading needle
* DMC seed beads, V1.10, Pearl white
* Three large ribbon roses, two pale blue, one mid blue
* Five small cream ribbon roses
* Two small cream pre-made bows
* String of pale blue pearl beads, 12in (30.5cm)
* Pale blue tassel
* Pale blue satin ribbon, 1½in (4cm) wide, 18in (46cm)
* White card, 6 x 8in (15 x 20cm)
* Tracing paper
* Sharp scissors
* Pencil
* Clear glue

1 Find the centre of the perforated paper by drawing a horizontal and a vertical line lightly in pencil, and begin stitching from the centre of the Slipper chart on page 53. Use two strands of cotton (floss) or a blend of two strands of cotton (floss) and one strand of Marlitt thread for the cross stitch as directed by the key. Use one strand for the backstitch outlining.

2 Using two strands of 368, stitch the leaves in lazy daisy stitch (see diagram opposite).

3 Stitch the scroll work and French knots in Kreinik fine braid. You will find it easier to sew with shorter lengths when using metallic thread.

4 Using four strands of Marlitt thread and following the chart, work long stitches to form the heart designs on the heel of the shoe. Attach a DMC seed bead in the centre of each flower with a half cross stitch in a single strand of 746 (see page 125).

5 When you have completed the stitching, trace the Slipper template on page 51 onto the card. Cut this shape out and lay it over the stitched piece. When you are happy with the position, lightly draw round it in pencil. Spread the back of the design with a thin layer of clear glue and stick it to the white card. Allow to dry before cutting round the pencil line with sharp scissors.

6 Stick the string of pale-blue pearl beads around the top edge of the slipper and across the heel, referring to the photograph for placement.

7 Fill the slipper with the blue and cream ribbon roses and stick into position with clear glue. Add the cream bows and tassel as shown.

8 Finish off by folding the blue satin ribbon in half and securing neatly to the back of the shoe with clear glue.

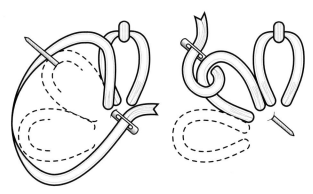

Lazy daisy stitch

Other Wedding Keepsakes

I hope my ideas will inspire you to create your own unique gifts – and other wedding keepsakes can be made using one or more elements from the sampler. You can have a lot of fun finding special ribbons and trimmings to use on a design, especially when you are making a keepsake to treasure. I made up the large box to resemble a wedding cake and stitched the dove design onto a pre-made Zweigart oval applique piece for the lid. The sides are adorned with the rose and ribbon scroll from the centre of the sampler. I stiffened these with needlework finisher, and cut them to shape before attaching them with clear glue. There is a huge choice of blank boxes available to decorate in this way. The roses appear again on a little pre-made aida bag for holding confetti or as a gift for a tiny bridesmaid. Finally, I used the initials from the sampler in a handsome box frame which I filled with wedding day keepsakes. Use pressed flowers from a bouquet, trimmings from the dress or other special reminders to complete this lovely item.

◆

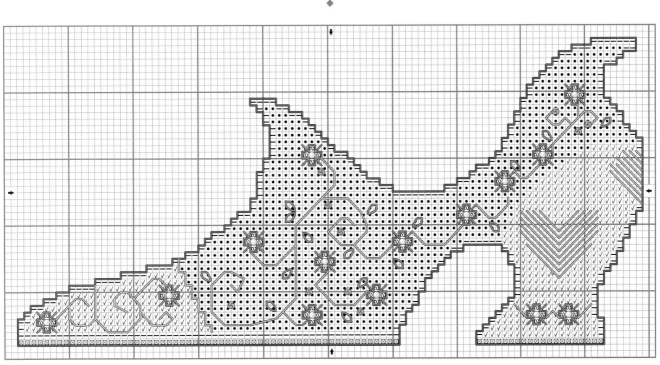

WEDDING SLIPPER

DMC

Cross stitch

√ √	Ecru + Marlitt 1012 (1)	
⊠ ⊠	613	Drab Brown - v lt
━ ━	739	Tan - ultra v lt
● ●	746	Off White
∽ ∽	775	Baby Blue - v lt

Backstitch

━━━	Kreinik Fine Braid	
	(08)221 – Antique Gold	
━━━	368	Pistachio Green - lt
━━━	3755	Baby Blue
━━━	611	Drab Brown

Long stitch

━━━	Marlitt 1012 (4)	

French knots

⑤	Kreinik Fine Braid	
	(08)221 - Antique Gold	

Beads

○	DMC seed beads	
	V1.10.Blanc - Pearl White	

Lazy daisy stitch

━━━	368	Pistachio Green - lt

STITCH NOTES

Stitched on perforated paper using two strands for cross stitch throughout. Blend with number of strands of Marlitt indicated in brackets. Backstitch in one strand. Long stitch in four strands.

A Boy and His Dog

'Friends are the sunshine of life'

T<small>HOMAS</small> H<small>AY</small>

*F*ew things endure longer than true friendship. Good friends accept us and our shortcomings without question. What better way to illustrate this than the special relationship between a boy and his pet. When I started to draw, the dog came first, a friendly old thing with his muzzle upturned and tail wagging. He needed someone to fuss his ears and pat his head. Who better than his young master – the sunshine of his doggy life! Stitched on sunny yellow aida, the warmth of the colours and the sentiment remind us that treasured friendships will brighten our lives long after their summer has passed.

◆

DESIGN SIZE: 7 x 5½in (18 x 14cm)
STITCH COUNT: 97 high x 77 wide

◆

YOU WILL NEED

• Lemon 14-count aida, 10 x 12in (25.5 x 30.5cm)
• DMC stranded cotton (floss) as listed in the key
• Tapestry needle, size 24
• Button or charm (optional)
• Clear glue

1 Find the centre of the fabric by folding it in half lengthways and widthways. Mark the folds with tacking (basting) stitches if desired, and begin stitching the chart on page 56 in the centre. Work the cross stitch in two strands of cotton (floss) and the backstitch in one strand.

2 When you have completed all the stitching check that you have not overlooked any areas of the design. Press your work and prepare it for framing following the instructions on page 126.

3 Glue the button or charm to your finished frame if you are using one.

T<small>HIS DESIGN IS IN THE STYLE MADE FAMOUS BY</small> <small>ONE OF MY FAVOURITE ILLUSTRATORS,</small> N<small>ORMAN</small> R<small>OCKWELL</small>, <small>ON THE MANY FRONT COVERS HE PRODUCED FOR THE</small> S<small>ATURDAY</small> E<small>VENING</small> P<small>OST</small>. F<small>OR THIS REASON</small> I <small>WANTED IT TO LOOK AS IF IT HAD BEEN CUT FROM THE MAGAZINE AND</small> I <small>LEFT VERY LITTLE FABRIC SHOWING AROUND THE DESIGN.</small>

A BOY AND HIS DOG

DMC

Cross stitch

• 01 White	– 712 Cream	– 930 Antique Blue - dk	↑ 3782 Mocha Brown - lt
● 310 Black	/ 727 Topaz - v lt	X 932 Antique Blue - lt	▪ 3787 Brown Grey - dk
T 355 Terracotta - dk	→ 738 Tan - v lt	+ 945 Tawny	Ɛ 3820 Straw - dk
⊠ 356 Terracotta - med	◇ 739 Tan - ultra v lt		951 Tawny - lt	
エ 433 Brown Golden - med	4 758 Terracotta - v lt	▽ 3022 Brown Grey - med	**Backstitch**
▲ 435 Brown Golden - v lt	◢ 838 Beige Brown - v dk	▶ 3023 Brown Grey - lt	—— 838 Beige Brown - v dk
J 437 Tan - lt	❖ 898 Coffee Brown - v dk	1 3024 Brown Grey - v lt	═══ 725 Topaz
θ 646 Beaver Grey - dk	D 924 Grey Green - v dk	▽ 3032 Mocha Brown - med	
▢ 647 Beaver Grey - med	N 926 Grey Green - med	Z 3773 Desert Sand - med	**French knots**
◇ 648 Beaver Grey - lt	◇ 927 Grey Green - lt	△ 3778 Mahogany - lt	● 898 Coffee Brown - v dk

STITCH NOTES

Stitched on 14-count aida using two strands for cross stitch. Backstitch and French knots in one strand.

The Gardener's Prayer

'The kiss of the sun for pardon
The song of the birds for mirth
You are nearer God's heart in a garden
Than anywhere else on earth'

This lovely little verse is often seen engraved upon sun dials and garden ornaments. I've used it as the centrepiece for a beautiful cushion which would be ideal for a conservatory. I love knot gardens with their box hedging and topiary trees and my favourite flower is lavender, so I have combined these elements in a garden of stitches. Entered through a wrought-iron gate, this garden is full of brick pathways lined with neat beds of dark green box and sweet-smelling lavender, leading to the magnificent bay tree. Two mother-of-pearl buttons in the shape of tiny birds add the finishing touch to this design which is complemented by a crisp cotton frill. Smaller projects such as scented sachets, a jar lacy and a bookmark, can all be made using details from the main cushion design.

◆

The Cushion

This versatile design forms the basis of all the other projects shown in this chapter. The project is simple to stitch and contains very few fractional stitches.

◆

DESIGN SIZE: 7⅞ x 8in (20 x 20.5cm)
STITCH COUNT: 110 wide x 113 high

◆

YOU WILL NEED

- Pale lavender 14-count aida, 14 x 14in (35.5 x 35.5cm)
- Cotton fabric for backing and frill, 21 x 48in (53 x 122cm)
- DMC stranded cotton (floss) as listed in the key
- Bond Multi's embellishment yarn, Gemstone
- Tapestry needle, size 24
- Cushion pad, 12in (30cm)
- Two small mother-of-pearl bird buttons or similar (optional)

1 Find the centre of the aida by folding it in half lengthways and widthways. Mark the folds with a line of tacking (basting) stitches if desired. Stitch the design from the Gardener's Prayer chart on pages 60–61, beginning in the centre. Use two strands of cotton (floss) for the cross stitch and one strand for the backstitch except for the lettering and the gate, which are sewn in two strands. Work the French knots in one strand.

2 A space-dyed thread has been used to enhance some of the flower beds. However, you can replace this with a stranded cotton colour or a different embellishing thread if you prefer.

3 When all the stitching is complete, add the buttons if you are using them, referring to the picture for placement.

4 Trim the stitched piece so that it measures 12 x 12in (30.5 x 30.5cm) and press (see page 126).

5 Cut one 12 x 12in (30.5 x 30.5cm) piece of cotton fabric for the backing. Cut two 4⅓in (11cm) strips across the width of the cotton fabric for the frill. Join the ends of these strips with ¼in (6mm) seams to form a circle. With wrong sides together, fold the strip in half and press. Sew a line of gathering stitches along the open edge and pull up to fit round the four sides of the stitched piece (front).

6 Pin the gathered frill around the edges of the front on the right side. Ensure the gathers are evenly distributed for a neat finish and tack (baste) in place.

7 With right sides together, place the back onto the front (ensuring the gathers are lying flat and to the centre of the work). Pin and sew a ½in (13mm) seam all round, leaving an opening at the bottom for turning. Trim the seams and clip the corners. Turn the right way out, insert the cushion pad and neatly slipstitch the opening.

Creating New Designs

It is very easy to take elements from the Gardener's Prayer chart to create your own unique items. All you need for this is several sheets of graph paper, a pencil, and most important, a little patience! Turn to page 126 for directions on how to chart your own designs. To inspire you I have made up several little items from the main chart, but you can probably come up with many more ways of your own for using this design.

◆

The knotwork cushion can be the starting point for many new designs like the ones shown here: A bookmark stitched on sea-green 28-count Meran evenweave, stiffened with plastic canvas and attached to a backing of antiqued leather. The sachets are stitched on green or lavender 28-count Meran and trimmed with contrasting silk cord looped at the corners. A button in the shape of a terracotta planter was perfect to hold the bay tree from the main design. Beads were substituted for some of the stitching on the green sachet. Stitching some of the motifs on a ready-made 18-count jar lacy makes a nice quick project, too.

The kiss of the sun
for pardon
The song of the birds
for mirth
You are nearer
God's heart
in a garden
than anywhere
else on earth

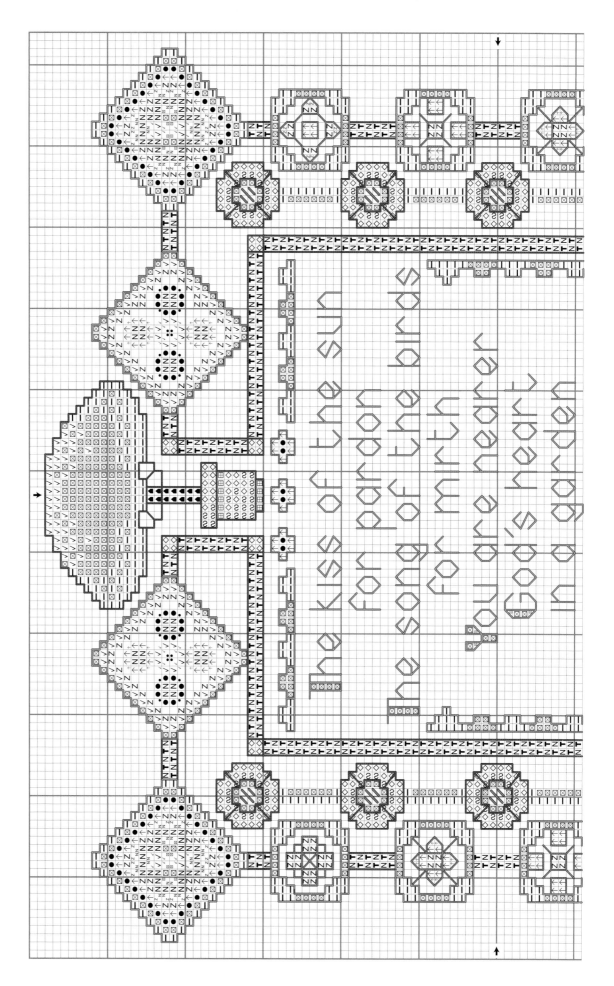

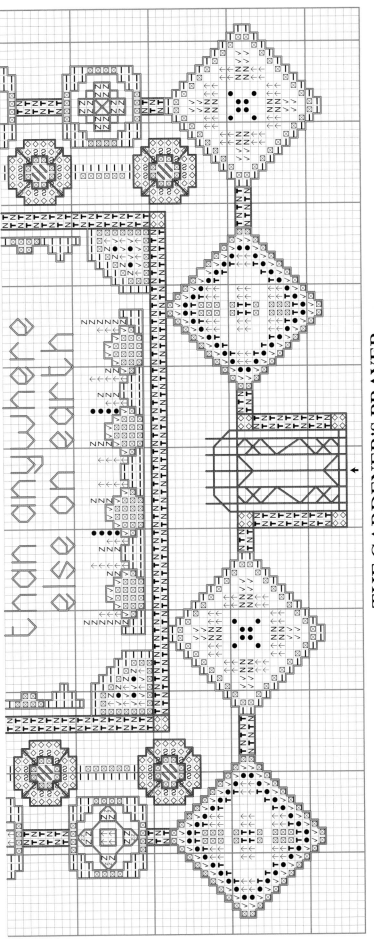

THE GARDENER'S PRAYER

T	920	Copper - med
N	922	Copper - lt
▨		Bond Multi Embellishment Yarn - Gemstone

Backstitch

——	550	Violet
——	561	Jade - v dk
——	838	Beige Brown - v dk

DMC

Cross stitch

●	550	Violet - v dk
↑	553	Violet
Z	554	Violet - lt
–	561	Jade - v dk
⊠	562	Jade - med
V	563	Jade - lt
⊞	611	Drab Brown
⊘	612	Drab Brown - lt
◇	613	Drab Brown - v lt
▲	838	Brown Beige - v dk

The Fisherman's Prayer

Dear God be good to me,
my boat is so small and the sea so wide...

FISHERMAN'S PRAYER

Of all the forces in nature, few are more formidable than the power of the sea. Sailors and seafarers know its many moods and their folklore and traditions reflect the need to respect them. My own great-grandfather, master of the Pilot Cutter that guided ships through the treacherous waters of the Bristol Channel, was lost at sea. Despite increasingly sophisticated methods of navigation and satellite tracking, the lighthouse continues to remain a steadfast symbol on our shores. The religious analogy is obvious. As times we all need a light in the darkness to steer us from danger and guide us into safe waters. So in my design I have chosen to combine the simple words of a traditional fisherman's prayer with a lighthouse dramatically silhouetted by a magnificent sunset. The warm shade of the apricot evenweave fabric is a perfect background for throwing the dark mass of rocky headland and the tiny sailing dinghy into sharp relief.

◆

DESIGN SIZE: 5¾ x 8⅛in (14.5 x 20.5cm)
STITCH COUNT: 81 wide x 114 high

◆

YOU WILL NEED

- Apricot 28-count evenweave, 12 x 14in (30.5 x 35.5cm)
- DMC stranded cotton (floss) as listed in the key
- Tapestry needle, size 26
- Mount board, 10 x 12in (25.5 x 30.5cm)
- Picture frame of your choice

1 Find the centre of your fabric by folding it in half lengthways and widthways. Mark each fold with a line of tacking (basting) stitches if desired. Find the centre of the chart on pages 64–65 and start stitching from here.

2 Work the design over two threads of the fabric using two strands of cotton (floss) for the cross stitch and one strand for the backstitch and French knots.

3 The clouds and sky are worked in half cross stitch using two strands. This is listed separately in the key and allocated a different symbol on the chart, but you will need to study the chart and key carefully because some shades are used for both full and half cross stitch.

4 When you have completed all the stitching, press your work and prepare it for framing (see page 126).

dear God be good
to me, my boat is
so small and the
sea so wide...
FISHERMAN'S PRAYER

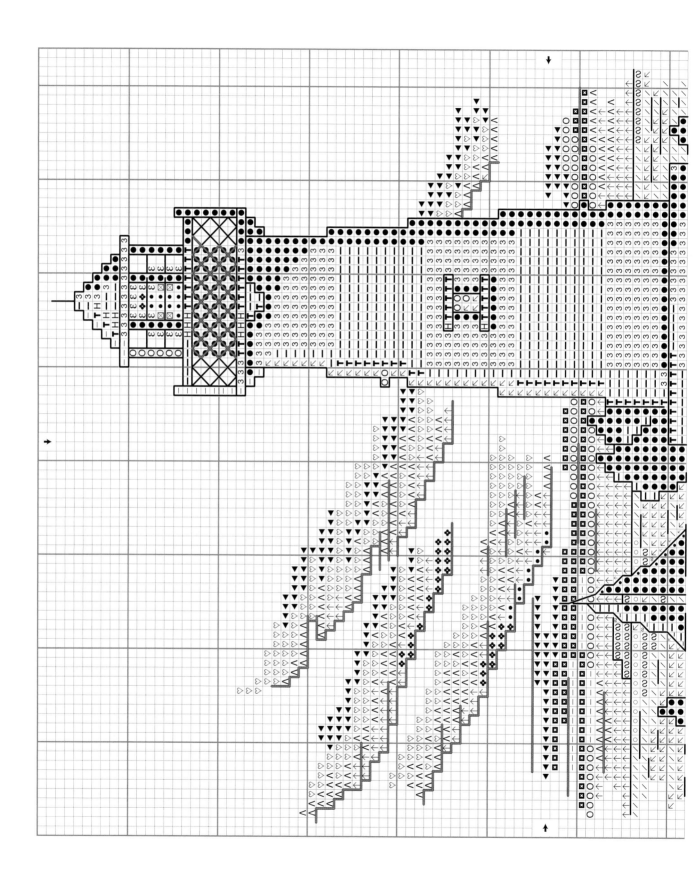

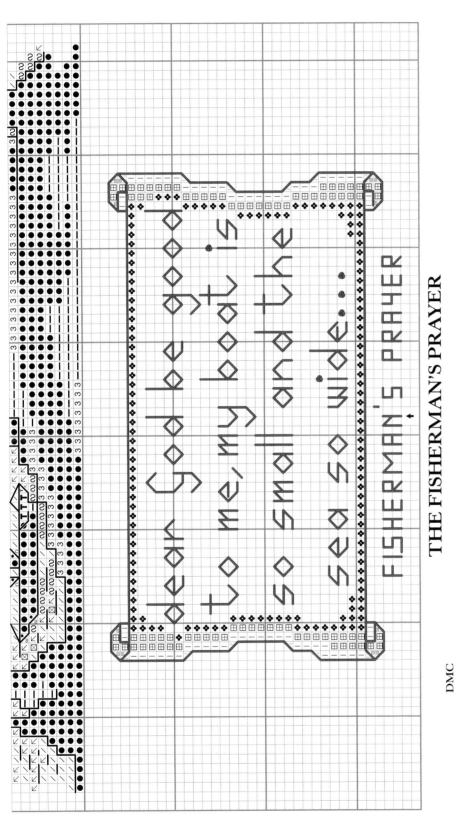

THE FISHERMAN'S PRAYER

Dear God be good to me, my boat is so small and the sea so wide . . .

FISHERMAN'S PRAYER

DMC

Cross stitch

·	01	White
●	310	Black
T	317	Silver Grey
H	318	Silver Grey - lt
—	413	Silver Grey - dk
2	608	Bright Orange
↖	722	Orange Spice - lt
ε	725	Topaz
/	740	Tangerine
○	741	Tangerine - med
⊠	744	Yellow - pale
✦	746	OffWhite
⊞	3033	Mocha Brown - v lt
		3782	Mocha Brown - lt
3	3799	Pewter Grey - v dk

Half cross stitch

▼	451	Silver Grey - dk
▽	452	Silver Grey - med
■	608	Bright Orange
∧	722	Orange Spice - lt
○	740	Tangerine
–	741	Tangerine - med
↑	744	Yellow - pale

Backstitch

—	310	Black
—	451	Silver Grey - dk
—	741	Tangerine - med
—	838	Beige Brown - v dk

French knots

●	838	Beige Brown - v dk

STITCH NOTES

Stitched over two threads on 28-count evenweave using two strands for cross stitch and half cross stitch. Backstitch in one strand. French knots in one strand.

Autumn
FULFILMENT

The season of mists and mellow fruitfulness is my own personal favourite. There is something very special about bright Autumn days that bear the first chill of Winter in the air. I associate swishing through fallen leaves, smelling woodsmoke in the air and planning Christmas projects with this lovely season.

We hope these will be halcyon days in the autumn of our life cycle. With our families grown, we look forward to having more time to pursue our own interests. And in this section you will find plenty of projects to occupy the shortening days. Stitch a jolly scarecrow couple, complete with corncob and toadstool buttons, to cheer up your kitchen or dining room. There is an intriguing project to illustrate the 'fruits of the spirit' listed in the Book of Galatians; it is sure to be a talking point. Or if you like to give gifts of preserves, you will find quick-to-stitch borders for making jars of jam and honey look extra special.

What could be a better gift for someone who is retiring than a clock, especially when it's a beautifully-stitched one? I based my design for the retirement clock in this section on the medieval Book of Hours. Finally, a simple harvest design is given a country look with a padded frame of crisp cotton checks, and you can stitch the tiny mouse to line the lid of a poppy-red trinket box.

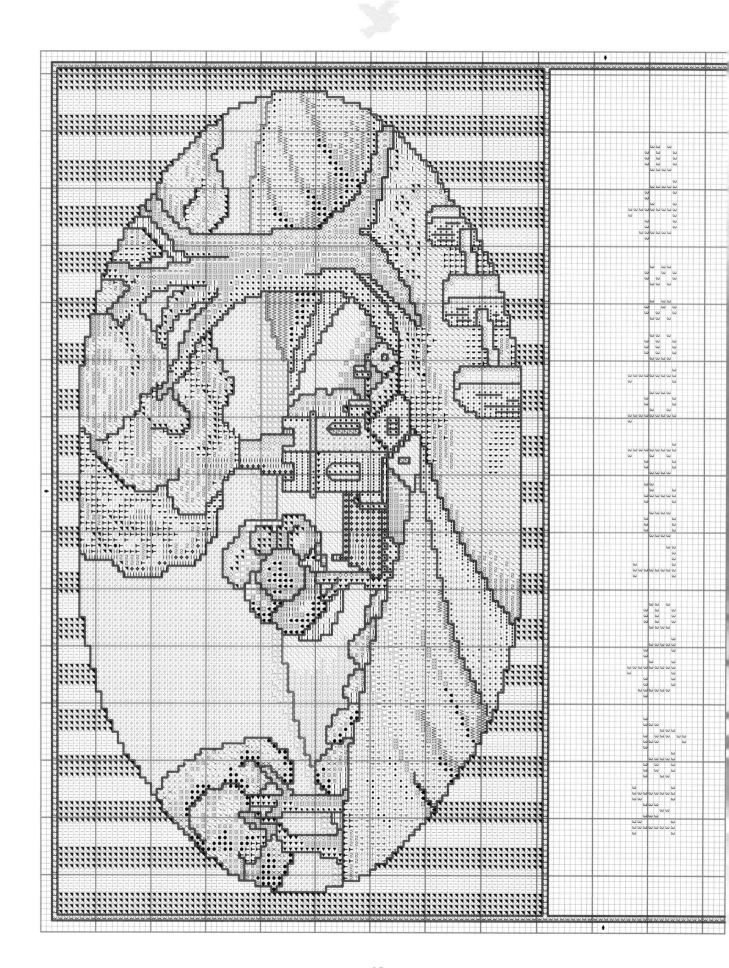

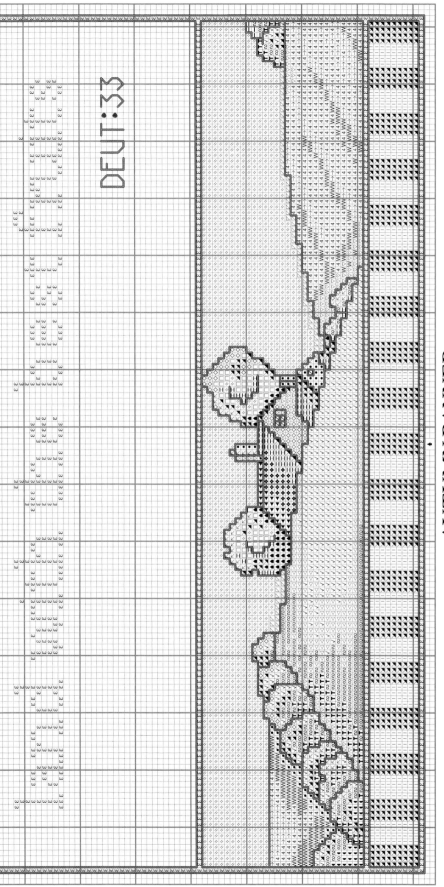

DEUT:33

AUTUMN BANNER

STITCH NOTES

Stitched on 14-count aida using two strands for cross stitch and half cross stitch throughout. Backstitch and French knots in one strand. DMC stranded cottons (floss) used throughout. One skein of each colour is required except for 747 and 3776 (2 skeins).

DMC

Cross stitch

□ 01	White
♣ 300	Mahogany - v dk
H 301	Mahogany - med
◀ 370	Mustard - med
⊠ 371	Mustard
□ 372	Mustard - lt
◇ 402	Mahogany - v lt
◼ 434	Brown Golden - lt
◻ 435	Brown Golden - v lt
X 471	Avocado Green - v lt
⊞ 611	Drab Brown
9 612	Drab Brown - lt
◇ 613	Drab Brown - v lt
⠂⠂ 646	Beaver Grey - dk
✳ 647	Beaver Grey - med
← 648	Beaver Grey - lt
→ 676	Golden Sand - lt
· 677	Golden Sand - v lt
WW 680	Golden Sand - dk
4 729	Golden Sand - med
◖ 730	Olive Green - v dk
T 731	Olive Green - dk
∂ 732	Olive Green
▽ 733	Olive Green - med
√ 734	Olive Green - lt
Z 740	Tangerine
— 829	Golden Olive - v dk

▼ 838	Beige Brown - v dk
Ɛ 931	Antique Blue - med
◤ 977	Rust - lt
▽ 3041	Silver Plum - med
⟋ 3042	Silver Plum - lt
◥ 3776	Mahogany - lt
◖ 3787	Brown Grey - dk

Half cross stitch

⊠ 747	Sky Blue - v lt
⊡ 3823	Yellow - ultra pale

Backstitch

— 680	Golden Sand - dk
— 838	Beige Brown - v dk
— 938	Coffee Brown - ultra dk
— 3041	Silver Plum - med

French knots

● 838	Beige Brown - v dk

Autumn Hanging Banner

Sometimes I think it is possible to feel the exact moment in time when a season turns. We've all stepped outside at the end of Summer and caught the first subtle scent of Autumn in the air. Although I live in a suburb of an industrial town, I can still see trees and farmland from the window of the room where I work. There are four large trees on my horizon that I especially love to watch for the first signs of the changing seasons, and they guide me through the year. I have tried to make each of these banners a 'snapshot' of the perfect day that typifies each season. Here is one of those days – a golden afternoon at the point where Summer slips into Autumn. We may mourn the passing of the longer days but the dedicated cross stitcher can always see the bright side of those cosy Autumn evenings!

◆

DESIGN SIZE : 10¾ x 14⅝in (27.5 x 37cm)
STITCH COUNT: 151 wide x 205 high

◆

YOU WILL NEED
* Cream 14-count aida, 15 x 18in (38 x 46cm)
* White cotton fabric for backing and tabs, 19½in (50cm)
* DMC stranded cotton (floss) as listed in the key
* Tapestry needle, size 24
* Silk cord, 2¼yds (2m)
* Large wooden bell-pull or doweling and wooden knobs for hanging

1 Find the centre of your fabric by folding it in half lengthways and widthways. Mark these folds with two lines of tacking (basting) stitches if desired. Starting from the centre, stitch the Autumn banner from the chart on pages 68–69, using two strands of stranded cotton (floss) for the cross stitch and one strand for the backstitch. Some areas of this design are stitched in half cross stitch using two strands to give the effect of a receding background. These are listed separately in the key.

2 Follow the key carefully when working the backstitch outlines because several different colours are used to give the project depth and clarity. Work the French knots in one strand.

3 When you have completed all the stitching, wash and press your work following the instructions on page 126.

4 Turn to page 14 for directions on how to make up your design into a banner.

◆

The Corn That Makes the Holy Bread

The corn that makes the holy Bread by which the soul of man is fed;
The holy Bread, the food unpriced, thy everlasting mercy, Christ.

JOHN MASEFIELD

Somehow the warmth of the golden days of an Indian summer is more special than the heat of high summer, perhaps because it has a bittersweet quality. We know that winter is around the corner. The farmer values good weather at this time of year to bring in the harvest. In this simple design I combined the words of the poet John Masefield with the theme of the harvest. In one corner are the fruits of the season in the shape of ripe pumpkins and cornstalks. In the other are the fruits of our labour represented by flour sacks and a bread crock filled with loaves. The gold communion chalice reminds us we cannot live by bread alone.

♦

Framed Picture

DESIGN SIZE: 7⅛ x 8¼in (18 x 21cm)
STITCH COUNT: 100 wide x 115 high

♦

YOU WILL NEED

* Parchment 28-count evenweave, 12 x 14in (30.5 x 35.5cm)
* DMC stranded cotton (floss) as listed in the key
* Tapestry needle, size 26
* DMC beads, V1.02.666, Christmas red; V1.06.741, Tangerine; V2.10 Blanc; V2.02.3777, Dark red; V4.02.666, Red; V4.05.3740, Mauve (optional)
* Beading needle
* Painted butterflies (optional)
* Checked cotton fabric, two 18 x 18in (46 x 46cm) pieces
* Red silk cord, 2¼yds (2m)
* Thick wadding (batting), 16 x 15in (40.5 x 38cm)
* Masking tape, 4cm wide
* Double-sided tape
* Mount board or thick card, two 15 x 14in (38 x 35.5cm) pieces
* Pencil and ruler
* Craft knife
* Clear glue
* Brass ring for hanging

1 Find the centre of your fabric by folding it in half lengthways and widthways. Find the centre of the chart on pages 74–75 and begin stitching from here.

2 Work the design over two threads of the fabric using two strands of cotton (floss) for the cross stitch and one strand for the backstitch. Work the French knots to show the seeds on the loaves in one strand. I used beads for my poppies, but this is optional. If you wish to do the same, substitute beads for the cotton (floss) colours listed in the Stitch Notes on page 75. Attach a bead for each symbol on the chart using a half cross (see page 125).

3 When you have completed all the stitching, wash and press your work (see page 126).

TO MAKE THE FRAME

1 First make the front. Draw an 8½ x 9½in (21.5 x 24cm) opening in the centre of one piece of card and cut this out with a craft knife.

♦

2 Place this cutout piece of card centrally over the wadding (batting) and use it as a template to cut out the centre of the wadding. Put this piece to one side – you will need it later to pad the stitched piece. Trim the remaining wadding (batting) to the size of the card frame and stick it down with double-sided tape.

3 Place the card, padded side down, over the wrong side of the cotton fabric. Fold the surplus fabric over to the back and stick down using masking tape. At this stage the opening in the centre will be covered by fabric.

4 Cut a small slit in the cotton fabric covering the opening in the centre. Then carefully cut diagonal lines from this slit to each corner. Turn these triangles of fabric to the back of the frame and tape in place.

5 Now make the back. Centre the second piece of card

on the wrong side of the remaining fabric. Turn over the surplus to the back and tape in place. Still with this side facing, use double-sided tape to stick the piece of wadding (batting) cut out from the front opening to the centre of the card. Use the front of the frame as a template to position this correctly.

6 Centre the stitching over the wadding (batting) on the back piece and carefully stick down.

7 Place the fabric-covered back and front pieces together and slip stitch neatly all round the edges. Finish off by whipstitching the silk cord to the edge of the frame using a dab of clear glue to prevent the cut ends from fraying.

8 Stitch the brass hanging ring to the back. If using butterflies or other embellishment, stick these in place using clear glue.

Trinket Box

The tiny harvest mouse makes a perfect subject for the lid of a trinket box which echoes the red poppies of his natural habitat. If you stitch the design on pale blue aida, none of the sky needs to be stitched.

◆

DESIGN SIZE: 1½ x 1½in (4 x 4cm)
STITCH COUNT: 20 wide x 20 high

◆

YOU WILL NEED

• Pale blue 14-count aida, 4 x 4in (10 x 10cm)
• DMC stranded cotton (floss) as listed in the key
• Tapestry needle, size 24
• Red enamel trinket pot, 32mm (Framecraft)

1 Find the centre of your fabric as usual. Find the circle containing the mouse design on the chart on page 74. Now find the centre of this motif by counting down 10 squares from the top and then 10 squares from the left-hand side. You may wish to mark lightly in pencil where these two points meet as a guide.

2 Begin stitching the design from this point using two strands for the cross stitch and one strand for the

backstitch outlining. You won't need to stitch the areas of 519 if you are using pale blue aida.

3 When you have completed all the stitching, wash and press your work (see page 126) and assemble it in the lid of the trinket box following the instructions provided.

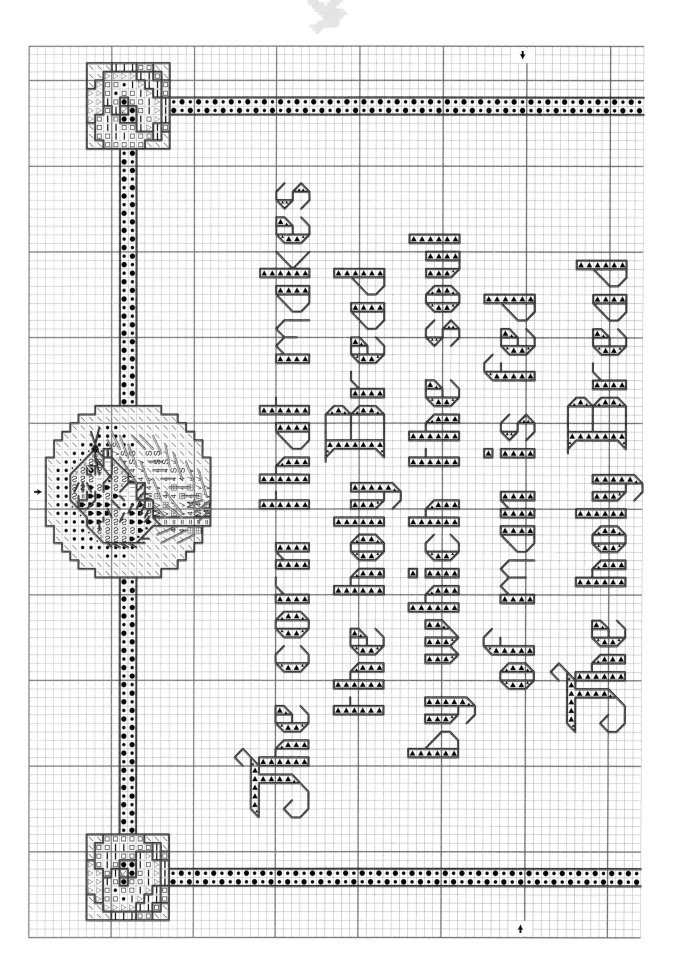

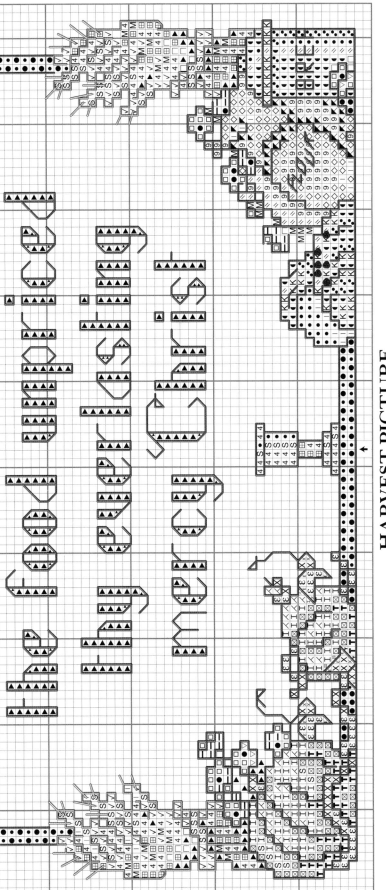

HARVEST PICTURE

STITCH NOTES

Stitched over two threads on 28-count evenweave using two strands for cross stitch and one strand for backstitch and French knots. Substitute DMC beads for the following colours if preferred: 01 with V2.10.Blanc; 321 with V2.02.3777 Dark Red; 351 with V4.02.666 Scarlet Red; 742 with V1.06.741 Tangerine; 3371 with V4.05.3740 Mauve; 3801 with V1.02.666 Christmas Red. Attach with a half cross.

DMC

Cross stitch

·	01	White
I	722 + 744 (1 of each)	
		Orange Spice + Yellow
–	321	Christmas Red
▷	351	Peach
▲	370	Mustard - med
M	371	Mustard
□	372	Mustard - lt
◖	434	Brown Golden - lt
◖	435	Brown Golden - v lt
K	437	Tan - lt
∠	519	Sky Blue
◤	611	Drab Brown
9	612	Drab Brown - lt
◇	613	Drab Brown - v lt
✓	676	Golden Sand - lt
S	677	Golden Sand - v lt
⊞	680	Golden Sand - dk
⊠	722	Orange Spice - lt
4	729	Golden Sand - med
⊠	739	Tan - ultra v lt
K	742	Tangerine - lt
⊠	744	Yellow Pale
I	746	Off White
◗	780	Topaz - ultra v dk
0	782	Topaz - dk
T	921	Copper
=	950	Desert Sand - lt
ε	3363	Pine Green - med
X	3364	Pine Green
●	3371	Black Brown
□	3801	Christmas Red - lt

Backstitch

——	01	White
——	680	Golden Sand - dk
——	727	Topaz - v lt
——	838	Beige Brown - v dk

French knots

●	3371	Black Brown

Make Haste, Slowly!

Retirement marks the end of our working lives, but most people find their days fuller than ever before. Our children grown, we have the time to try new hobbies or travel to places we have always dreamed of. But whether we intend to do a spot of gardening or to write a great novel, what matters is that we make the most of our new-found free time. And perhaps this is why clocks and watches are traditionally given as retirement gifts. How much nicer, though, to own one that has been stitched. My retirement clock is based on floral designs from the medieval Books of Hours which seemed appropriate. It includes the Latin inscription 'Festina Lente' which appears on a plaque in the Vatican and means 'make haste, slowly'. If you have to make haste, simply stitch the pansy lattice design to line the lid of a handsome wooden bowl as a lovely quick gift.

◆

The Clock

DESIGN SIZE: 3¾ x 5⅝in (9.5 x 14cm)
STITCH COUNT: 53 wide x 79 high

◆

YOU WILL NEED

- Apricot 28-count evenweave, 9 x 11in (23 x 28cm)
- DMC stranded cotton (floss) as listed in the key
- Tapestry needle, size 26
- Sudberry House mantle clock (127mm x 177mm)
  (see page 127)

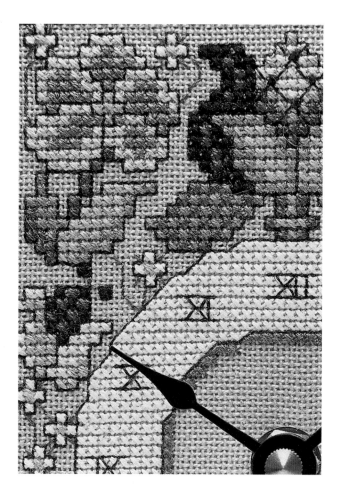

1 Find the centre of your fabric by folding it in half lengthways and widthways. Find the centre of the Retirement Clock chart on page 78 and begin stitching from here.

2 Work the design over two threads of the evenweave, using two strands of cotton (floss) for the cross stitch and one strand for the backstitch and French knots.

3 When you have completed the stitching, wash and press your work (see page 126) before assembling it in the clock following the instructions provided.

4 An alternative way of mounting this design as a clock is to frame it in a standard picture frame and add a clock mechanism you have bought separately.

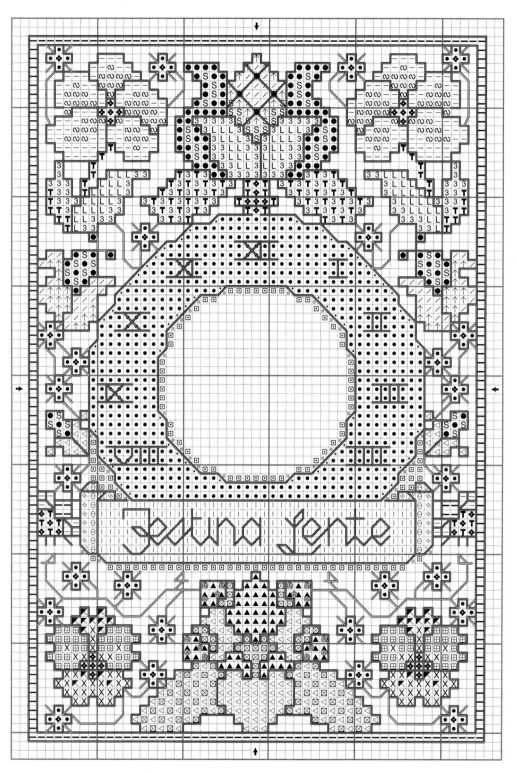

RETIREMENT CLOCK

DMC

Cross stitch

· ·	01	White
↑ ↑	224	Shell Pink - v lt
╱ ╱	225	Shell Pink - ultra v lt
▲ ▲	326	Rose - v dk
▏▏▏	712	Cream
⊠ ⊠	731	Olive Green - dk
◁ ◁	733	Olive Green -med
θ θ	738	Tan - v lt
╲ ╲	738	Tan - ultra v lt
● ●	814	Garnet - dk
▬ ▬	829	Golden Olive - v dk
T T	830	Golden Olive - dk
3 3	832	Golden Olive
L L	834	Golden Olive - v lt
∞ ∞	931	Antique Blue - med
◤ ◤	3041	Silver Plum - med
⊞ ⊞	3042	Silver Plum - lt
S S	3722	Shell Pink - med
X X	3743	Silver Plum - v lt
▬ ▬	3752	Antique Blue - v lt
▣ ▣	3776	Mahogany - lt
✤ ✤	3820	Straw - dk

Backstitch

━━━	731	Olive Green - dk
━━━	3031	Mocha Brown - v dk

French knots

●	814	Garnet - dk
◉	3820	Straw - dk

STITCH NOTES

Stitched over two threads on 28-count evenweave using two strands for cross stitch throughout, and one strand for backstitch and French knots.

Floral Lattice Trinket Box

DESIGN SIZE: 2¾ x 2⅝in (7 x 6.5cm)
STITCH COUNT: 39 wide x 37 high

◆

YOU WILL NEED

* Beige 14-count aida, 4 x 4in (10 x 10cm)
* DMC stranded cotton (floss) as listed in the key
* Elm-wood bowl 3in (8.9cm) (Framecraft)

1 Find the centre of your fabric by folding it in half lengthways and widthways. Find the centre of the Pansy Trellis chart below and begin stitching from here. Use two strands of cotton (floss) for the cross stitch and one strand for the backstitch.

2 When you have completed all the stitching, wash and press your work (see page 126) before assembling it in the lid of the bowl following the instructions provided.

PANSY TRELLIS

DMC
Cross stitch

·	·	01	White
◤	◥	3041	Silver Plum - med
⊞	⊞	3042	Silver Plum - lt
X	X	3743	Silver Plum - v lt
◆	◆	3820	Straw - dk

Backstitch

———	731	Olive Green - dk
———	3031	Mocha Brown - v dk

STITCH NOTES

Stitched on 14-count aida using two strands for cross stitch and one strand for backstitch.

◆

Mr and Mrs Scarecrow

*'Come ye thankful people come, raise the song of harvest home,
all is safely gathered in 'ere the winter storms begin...'*

TRADITIONAL HYMN

In many ways our lives echo the cycle of nature. The time and care we spend planting ideas and nurturing lasting values in our children will one day bear fruit. Hard work brings its own reward, enjoyed in the golden days of autumn, both of the season and in our lives. Scarecrows seemed a perfect symbol for this season and the celebration of harvest, and I set them among sunflowers, corn stalks, and berries for a really autumnal feeling. Buttons, a sunshine yellow raffia bow and matching blue-checked fabric provide special finishing touches. A hazel twig hanger completes the rustic theme.

◆

DESIGN SIZE: 8 x 11¼in (20.3 x 28.7cm)
STITCH COUNT: 112 wide x 158 high

◆

YOU WILL NEED

- 14-count Rustico aida, 12 x 14in (30 x 35.5.cm)
- DMC stranded cotton (floss) as listed in the key
- Blue cotton gingham, 20in (50cm)
- Buttons – 3 sunflowers, 4 toadstools and 2 corn cobs
- Hazel twig or similar, approx. 19in (48cm) long
- Pre-made yellow raffia bow

1 Find the centre of your fabric by folding it in half lengthways and widthways. Mark these folds with a line of tacking (basting) stitches if desired. Stitch the Mr and Mrs Scarecrow chart on pages 82–83 starting in the centre. Work the cross stitch and the long stitch detail on the corn stalks and the scarecrows' straw in two strands of cotton (floss). Use one strand for all other backstitch.

2 Add the corn stalks and toadstool buttons in the positions indicated on the chart using a single strand of matching cotton.

3 To make the wall-hanging, cut two 16 x 18in (41.3 x 46cm) pieces of gingham plus three more 6 x 4in (16.5 x 11.4cm) pieces for the tabs. Place the cross stitch over one of the large gingham pieces on the right side so that 2½in (6.35cm) of gingham is visible all round. Sew in place allowing about ½in (12mm) for fraying. Carefully remove one or two horizontal threads from the aida up to the stitching line.

4 To make the tabs fold each piece in half lengthways with right sides together. Sew a ¼in (6mm) seam down the length and form a point at one end. Trim the seam across the point for a neater finish. Turn the right way out and press.

5 Place the tabs on the right side of the front with the points towards the centre. Matching the raw edges, pin in place. Place the backing on top and with rights sides together stitch all round taking in the tabs and leaving a gap at the bottom for turning. Turn the right way out, press and slip stitch the opening. Pull the loose ends of the tabs to the front and secure each one with a sunflower button.

6 Stitch or stick on the yellow raffia bow or apply other trimming if preferred.

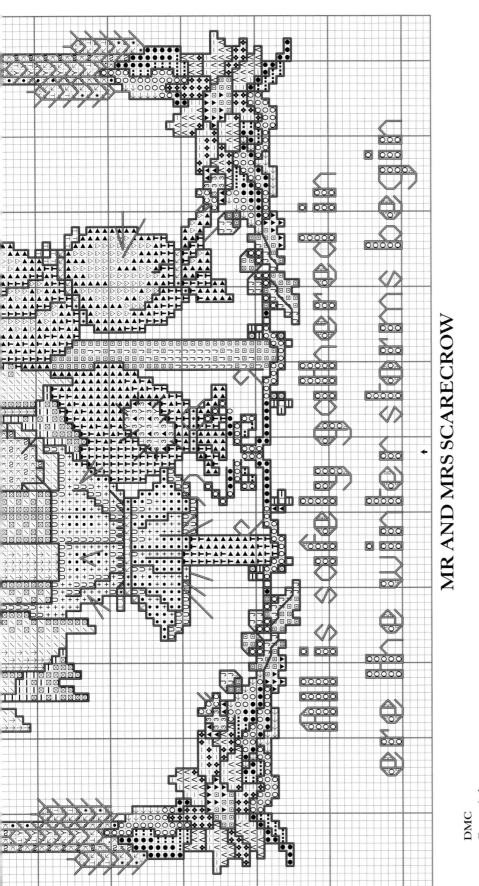

MR AND MRS SCARECROW

DMC

Cross stitch

●|•	01 White
□|□	350 Peach - med
↓|↓	353 Peach - v lt
⊠|⊠	356 Terracotta - med
▶|▼	433 Brown Golden - med
⊡|⊡	435 Brown Golden - v lt
J|J	437 Tan - lt
U|U	452 Shell Grey - med
□|□	453 Shell Grey - lt
+|+	469 Avocado Green
O|O	471 Avocado Green - v lt

←|←	472 Avocado Green - ultra v lt
▽|▽	642 Beige Grey - dk
⊥|⊥	676 Golden Sand - lt
Y|Y	677 Golden Sand - v lt
∗|∗	680 Golden Sand - dk
▲|▲	720 Orange Spice - dk
3|3	722 Orange Spice - lt
—|—	727 Topaz - v lt
↖|↖	729 Golden Sand - med
I|I	730 Olive Green - v dk
▽|▽	732 Olive Green

4|4	734 Olive Green - lt
—|—	815 Garnet - med
1|1	822 Beige Grey - lt
T|T	839 Beige Brown - dk
▲|▲	840 Beige Brown - med
▽|▽	841 Beige Brown - lt
⊤|⊤	842 Beige Brown - v lt
▼|▼	930 Antique Blue - dk
℧|℧	931 Antique Blue - med
K|K	932 Antique Blue - lt
⋮|⋮	937 Avocado Green - med

❖|❖	972 Canary - deep
△|△	973 Canary - bright
∕|∕	3341 Apricot
⊤|⊤	3752 Antique Blue - v lt
C|C	3825 Pumpkin - pale

Backstitch

—— 838 Beige Brown - v dk
—— 469 Avocado Green

Long stitch

—— 680 Golden Sand - dk

STITCH NOTES

Stitched on 14-count aida using two strands for cross stitch throughout. Backstitch in one strand. Long stitch details on corn ears and scarecrows' stuffing in two strands.

The Fruits of the Spirit

'Love, patience, loyalty, joy, goodness,
peace, courtesy and self-control'

I wanted to do a design of these eight 'fruits of the spirit' listed in the Book of Galatians but I knew it would be hard to illustrate such an abstract list of virtues. I started to doodle and drew a little wooden cabinet. Our neighbour, Mrs Brown, had a huge Welsh dresser in her home. It held her treasures and prized possessions, everything from huge china platters to tiny seaside souvenirs. As a child, I loved to climb on a chair and inspect them all. My favourite was the egg-timer – so it appears here to represent patience, along with a heart pin-cushion for love, a china dog for loyalty, an angel for joy, and a honey-pot for goodness. A folk-art dove shows us peace and an old sampler reminds us of the virtue of courtesy. That left me with one problem – how to illustrate self-control. So a delicious little chocolate cake sits uneaten on the shelf!

◆

Framed Picture

DESIGN SIZE: 7½ x 10¼in (19 x 27.5cm)
STITCH COUNT: 104 wide x 143 high

◆

YOU WILL NEED

* Antique cream 28-count evenweave, 14 x 17in
(30.5 x 38cm)
* DMC stranded cotton (floss) as listed in the key
* Tapestry needle, size 26
* Beading needle
* DMC seed beads, V1.10.5200, Matt white
* Mount board, 12 x 15in (30.5 x 38cm)
* Picture frame of your choice

1 Find the centre of your fabric by folding it in half lengthways and widthways. Begin stitching the Fruits of the Spirit chart on pages 86–87 from the centre. Work the design over two threads of the fabric using two strands of stranded cotton (floss) for the cross stitch and one strand for the backstitch outlining and French knots.

2 Some areas of shading are worked in half cross stitch using two strands and are listed separately in the key.

3 Attach each of the beads spread randomly over the top of the chocolate cake with a half cross stitch using one strand of white (see page 125).

4 When you have completed all the stitching, press your work and prepare it for framing (see page 126).

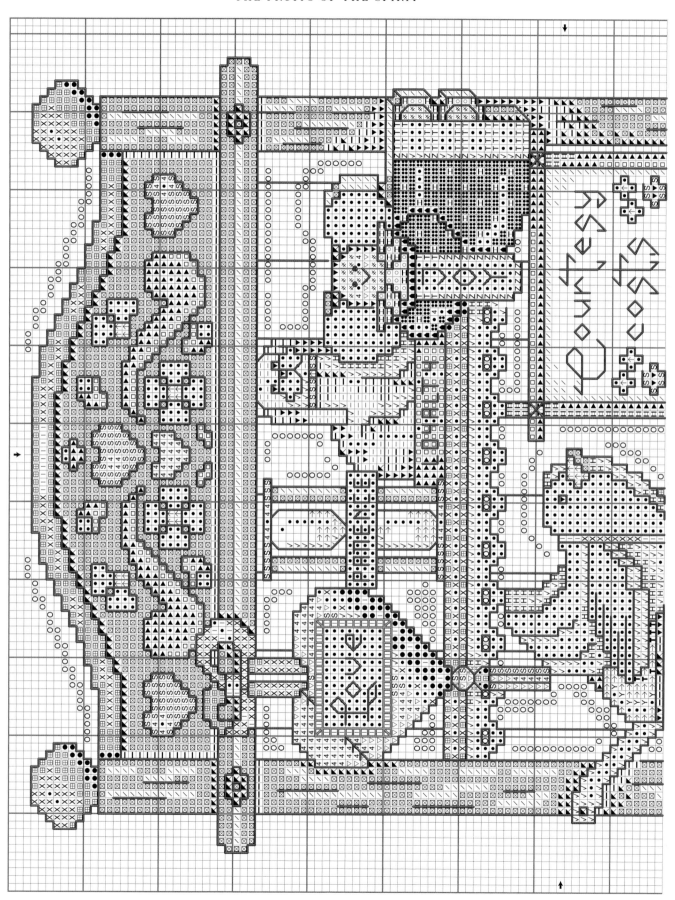

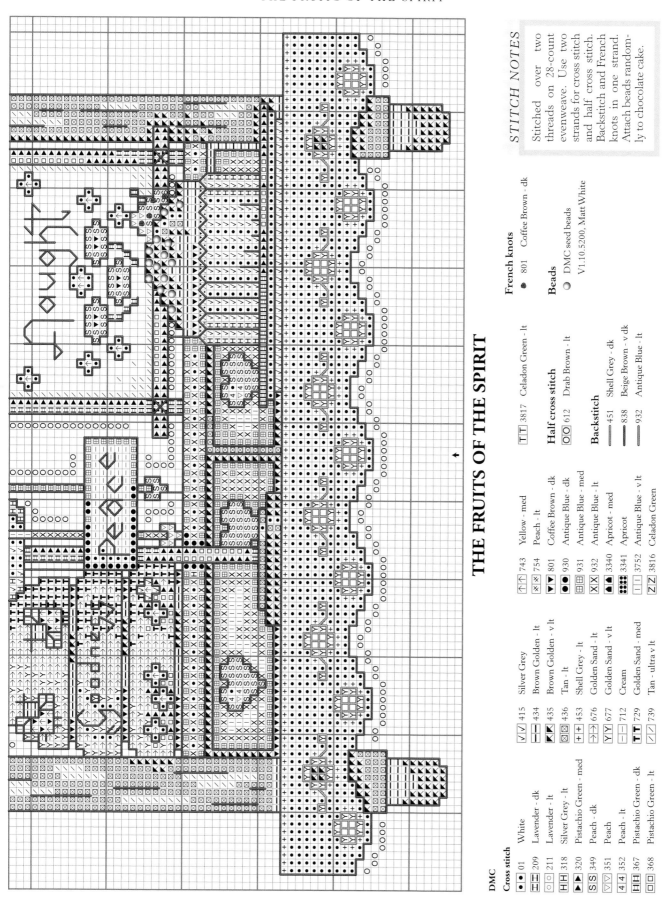

THE FRUITS OF THE SPIRIT

STITCH NOTES

Stitched over two threads on 28-count evenweave. Use two strands for cross stitch and half cross stitch. Backstitch and French knots in one strand. Attach beads randomly to chocolate cake.

French knots

● 801   Coffee Brown - dk

Beads

◐ DMC seed beads
V1.10.5200, Matt White

Half cross stitch

T T 3817   Celadon Green - lt

O O 612   Drab Brown - lt

Backstitch

——— 451   Shell Grey - dk

——— 838   Beige Brown - v dk

——— 932   Antique Blue - lt

DMC

Cross stitch

● ● 01	White	
H H 209	Lavender - dk	
○ ○ 211	Lavender - lt	
H H 318	Silver Grey - lt	
▲ ▲ 320	Pistachio Green - med	
S S 349	Peach - dk	
▽ ▽ 351	Peach	
4 4 352	Peach - lt	
H H 367	Pistachio Green - dk	
□ □ 368	Pistachio Green - lt	

V V 415	Silver Grey	
H H 434	Brown Golden - lt	
◣ ◣ 435	Brown Golden - v lt	
⊠ ⊠ 436	Tan - lt	
+ + 453	Shell Grey - lt	
▷ ▷ 676	Golden Sand - lt	
Y Y 677	Golden Sand - v lt	
– – 712	Cream	
T T 729	Golden Sand - med	
Z Z 739	Tan - ultra v lt	

↑ ↑ 743	Yellow - med	
✕ ✕ 754	Peach - lt	
▶ ▼ 801	Coffee Brown - dk	
● ● 930	Antique Blue - dk	
⊞ ⊞ 931	Antique Blue - med	
X X 932	Antique Blue - lt	
◀ ▲ 3340	Apricot - med	
⠿ ⠿ 3341	Apricot	
I I 3752	Antique Blue - v lt	
Z Z 3816	Celadon Green	

Border Motifs

There are many attractive aida and linen bands available for use with border designs. You can also use vinylweave, an easy-care fabric which is ideal for projects which come into contact with sticky fingers – for example, decorating jam and marmalade pots. All these borders are based on elements of The Fruits of the Spirit picture. Band 1 features the folk-art painting from the top of the little cupboard. Band 2 has fat bumble bees buzzing around their hives and would make a really pretty design for the edge of table napkins. Band 3 features a fresh blue-and-white checked border edging bunches of bright poppies and daisies. Band 4 would work well as a Christmas design for table linen. The arrows on the charts show the point at which the border patterns repeat. However, on band 3 I have not included the checked edging as part of the repeat. It is simpler to add this afterwards especially if you wish to alter the depth of this border. Why not experiment with different colour combinations for the flowers and the edging.

◆

◆

PRESERVE BANDS

DMC

Cross stitch

·	01	White	√	415	Silver Grey	▼	801	Coffee Brown

· 01	White	√ 415	Silver Grey	▼ 801	Coffee Brown
H 318	Silver Grey - lt	— 434	Brown Golden - lt	⊞ 931	Antique Blue - med
▶ 320	Pistachio Green - med	◤ 435	Brown Golden - v lt	X 932	Antique Blue - lt
S 349	Peach - dk	→ 676	Golden Sand - lt	I 3752	Antique Blue - v lt
▽ 351	Peach	Y 677	Golden Sand - v lt		
4 352	Peach - lt	— 712	Cream	**Backstitch**	
H 367	Pistachio Green - dk	T 729	Golden Sand - med	—— 838	Beige Brown - v dk
□ 368	Pistachio Green - lt	↑ 743	Yellow - med		

These quick-to-stitch border designs are in the same style as the Fruits of the Spirit picture on page 85. Stitched on vinylweave and 16-count Rustico aida bands using two strands for cross stitch and one strand for backstitch, they are ideal for decorating jars of preserves. You can also stitch them on a lower-count fabric to decorate tea towels, a tea cosy or for shelf edging.

𝔚inter
CONTENTMENT

𝒞hristmas is the bright spot in the darkness of winter. Preparing for it, baking, writing cards and, of course, stitching projects, is almost as much fun as the holiday itself. Now is the time of year when stitchers come into their own! Everything from tiny gift tags to magnificent tree skirts are made with the same loving care. The love of home and the warmth of the family circle are especially important at this time.

𝒯he winter banner shows the now familiar valley beneath a thick layer of snow glittering in the frosty moonlight. Stitch only the landscape at the top if this is your favourite season. Instead of a typical Santa, I decided to show the image of an equally friendly and smiling Saint Nicholas on a splendid shaped cushion. On the theme of home, the project 'Peace Be to This House' shows light spilling from the windows of a lovely house onto the cheerful snowman keeping guard outside. A set of jolly Victorian Villas can be used in many combinations to make cards, decorations or a lovely festive picture to hang up year after year.

𝔅ut the most important part of the season has not been forgotten. Experienced stitchers will relish the challenge of the intricate Celtic knotwork on the Gaelic Blessing Nativity projects. Or why not put the dark evenings to good use by stitching the 'Light of the World', a very special adaptation of a famous picture to take pride of place in your home throughout the year.

He spreads the snow
like wool. He scatters
the frost like ashes.

PSALM 147:16

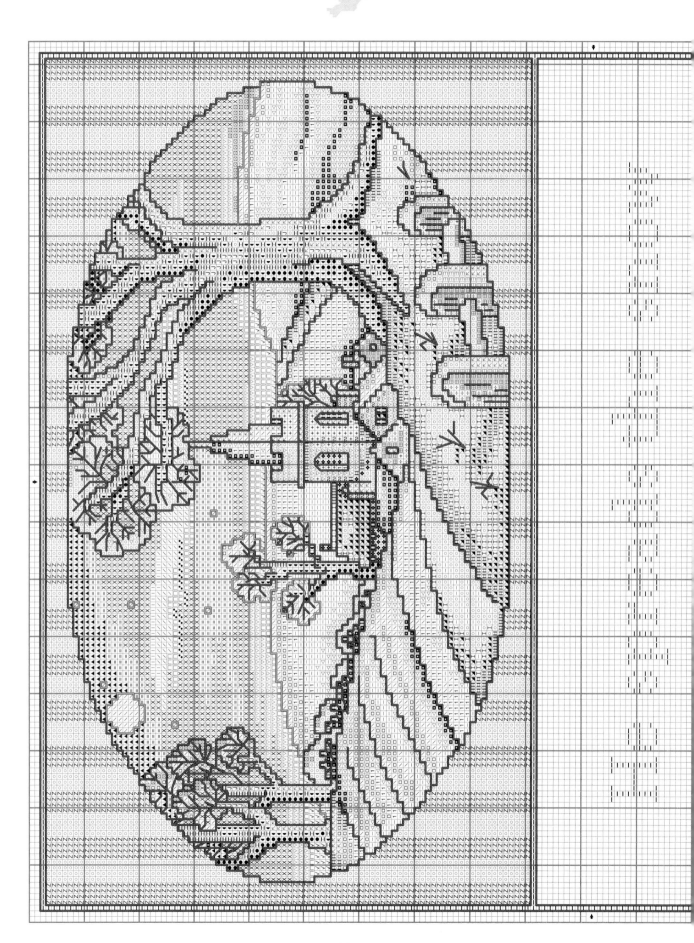

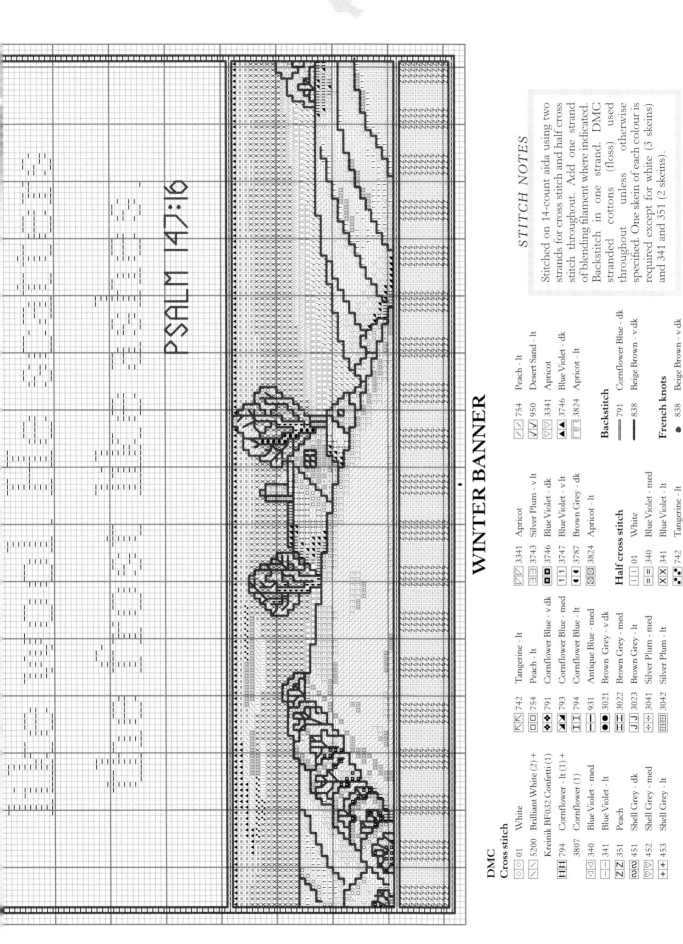

PSALM 147:16

WINTER BANNER

DMC

Cross stitch

01	White	
5200	Brilliant White (2) +	
	Kreinik BF032 Confetti (1)	
794	Cornflower - lt (1) +	
3807	Cornflower (1)	
340	Blue Violet - med	
341	Blue Violet - lt	
351	Peach	
451	Shell Grey - dk	
452	Shell Grey - med	
453	Shell Grey - lt	
742	Tangerine - lt	
754	Peach - lt	
791	Cornflower Blue - v dk	
793	Cornflower Blue - med	
794	Cornflower Blue - lt	
931	Antique Blue - med	
3021	Brown Grey - v dk	
3022	Brown Grey - med	
3023	Brown Grey - lt	
3041	Silver Plum - med	
3042	Silver Plum - lt	
3341	Apricot	
3743	Silver Plum - v lt	
3746	Blue Violet - dk	
3747	Blue Violet - v lt	
3787	Brown Grey - dk	
3824	Apricot - lt	
754	Peach - lt	
950	Desert Sand - lt	
3341	Apricot	
3746	Blue Violet - dk	
3824	Apricot - lt	

Half cross stitch

01	White	
340	Blue Violet - med	
341	Blue Violet - lt	
742	Tangerine - lt	

Backstitch

791	Cornflower Blue - dk
838	Beige Brown - v dk

French knots

● 838	Beige Brown - v dk

STITCH NOTES

Stitched on 14-count aida using two strands for cross stitch and half cross stitch throughout. Add one strand of blending filament where indicated. Backstitch in one strand. DMC stranded cottons (floss) used throughout unless otherwise specified. One skein of each colour is required except for white (3 skeins) and 341 and 351 (2 skeins).

Winter Hanging Banner

Here is the last, and perhaps the most picturesque, glimpse of the little valley. Now deep snow covers the fields, glittering in the frosty moonlight. Although the first of the evening stars has appeared, there is just enough afterglow of sunset to paint the western sky with orange light. This last fiery flare gives warmth to the otherwise chilly scene.In some ways this was the hardest design to create. I spent many hours trying to get the right play of light and shadow on the snow. After all, it is never just white, particularly in twilight, so I used a palette ranging from the deepest indigo to the palest apricot. In some areas the colours are blended to achieve the right effect and patches of snow have been given a frosty shimmer by the addition of blending filament. Although I had some initial misgivings about using such strong colours, I needn't have worried – nature is the greatest artist after all.

◆

DESIGN SIZE : 10¾ x 14⅝in (27.5 x 37cm)
STITCH COUNT: 151 wide x 205 high

◆

YOU WILL NEED

* Cream 14-count aida, 15 x 18in (38 x 46cm)
* White cotton fabric for backing and tabs, 19½in (50cm)
* DMC stranded cotton (floss) as listed in the key
* Kreinik Blending Filament, Shade 032, Confetti
* Tapestry needle, size 24
* Silk cord, 2¼yds (2m)
* Large wooden bell-pull or doweling and wooden knobs for hanging

using two strands of cotton (floss) for the cross stitch and one strand for the backstitch. Some areas of this design are stitched in half cross stitch using two strands to give the effect of a receding background. Others are worked in a blend of cotton (floss) and blending filament, or two different shades of stranded cotton (floss). These are all listed with separate symbols in the key.

1 Find the centre of your fabric by folding it in half lengthways and widthways. Mark this with two lines of tacking (basting) stitches if desired. Starting from the centre, stitch the Winter Banner chart on pages 92–93,

2 Follow the key carefully when working the backstitch because several colours are used to give the design depth.

3 When you have completed all the stitching, press your work (see page 126) and turn to page 14 for directions on how to make up the banner.

◆

The Children's Saviour

Long before the jolly figure of Santa Claus became associated with Christmas, children looked forward to a visit from Saint Nicholas. Saint Nicholas was a fourth-century bishop, who was famous for his benevolence and had a special affinity for children and the needy. Many countries including Russia adopted him as their patron saint and made the date of his death, 6th December, a feast day marking the beginning of Christmas. This is still observed in parts of Northern Europe today. Dressed in rich robes, my Saint Nicholas has the twinkling eyes and kindly smile of a familiar Santa. But instead of a sack of Christmas goodies, he carries his crook and wears a Bishop's mitre to remind us of his origin. Stitched on a large scale, he makes a splendid stuffed figure. Place him on a favourite chair during the festive season or stand him by your tree to keep a benevolent eye on the proceedings.

◆

DESIGN SIZE: 7 x 12½in (18 x 38cm)
STITCH COUNT: 70 wide x 125 high

◆

YOU WILL NEED

* Sage 19/20-count evenweave, 13 x 19in (33 x 48cm)
* Red cotton fabric for backing, 13 x 19in (33 x 48cm)
* DMC stranded cotton (floss) as listed in the key
* Tapestry needle, size 26
* Gold silk cord, 60in (1.5m)
* Good quality toy filling, about 8oz

1 Find the centre of your fabric by folding it in half lengthways and widthways. Mark this with two lines of tacking (basting) stitches if desired. Start stitching from the centre of the Saint Nicholas chart on pages 96–97. Work the design over two threads of the fabric using four strands of cotton (floss) for the cross stitch and two strands for the backstitch.

2 When you have completed all the stitching, wash and press your work (see page 126).

3 Following the shape of the Saint Nicholas figure, lightly mark a 2¼in (5.5cm) seam allowance all round the edge of the design in pencil. Carefully cut this out using sharp scissors. Pin the stitching on top of the backing material and cut the backing to the same shape as the stitched front.

4 With right sides together, pin and sew a ¼in (6mm) seam all round, leaving an opening at the base. Turn the cushion the right way out and stuff firmly. Slip stitch the opening together and trim by whipstitching the gold cord around the edge. Apply a small dab of clear glue on the cord ends to prevent fraying.

TIP

I MADE MY SAINT NICHOLAS LARGER BY STITCHING HIM OVER TWO THREADS OF 19/20-COUNT EVENWEAVE. IF YOU WANT TO REDUCE HIM IN SIZE, TRY STITCHING THE DESIGN ON 14-COUNT AIDA OR AN EVEN HIGHER COUNT FABRIC. YOU COULD ALSO WORK OVER ONE THREAD OF THE 19/20-COUNT EVENWEAVE. ADD BEADS OR ANY OTHER SPECIAL THREADS TO GIVE EXTRA SPARKLE, OR STITCH HIM ON A MIDNIGHT BLUE OR BLACK FABRIC TO SHOW OFF THE RICH COLOURS ON HIS ROBES. ALTERNATIVELY, WHY NOT WORK THE DESIGN ON 10-COUNT CANVAS USING TAPESTRY WOOL TO MAKE A REALLY BEAUTIFUL NEEDLEPOINT CUSHION.

SAINT NICHOLAS

DMC

Cross stitch

· ·	01	White
✳ ✳	310	Black
T T	333	Blue Violet - v dk
C C	340	Blue Violet - med
⊠ ⊠	349	Peach - dk
W W	351	Peach
− −	433	Brown Golden - med
▣ ▣	435	Brown Golden - v lt
I I	437	Tan - lt
♡ ♡	452	Silver Grey - med
√ √	453	Silver Grey - lt
◭ ◭	553	Violet
K K	554	Violet - lt
⊞ ⊞	580	Moss Green - dk
Ɛ Ɛ	581	Moss Green
X X	725	Topaz
↑ ↑	727	Topaz - v lt
S S	783	Topaz - med
◤ ◢	814	Garnet - dk
◖ ◖	830	Golden Olive - dk
⫟ ⫟	831	Golden Olive - med
⣿ ⣿	832	Golden Olive
O O	834	Golden Olive - v lt
÷ ÷	3746	Blue Violet - dk
J J	3773	Desert Sand - med
○ ○	3774	Desert Sand - v lt
− −	3823	Yellow - ultra pale

Backstitch

▬▬	838	Beige Brown - v dk

STITCH NOTES

Stitched over two threads on 19/20-count evenweave using four strands for cross stitch and two strands for backstitch. DMC stranded cottons (floss) used through-out. One skein of each colour is required except for white and 349 (2 skeins).

Peace Be to This House

*This simple quotation from Luke 10:5 was my
starting point for this welcoming design. I chose a
lovely royal blue evenweave as a background fabric
for the way it brings out the contrast of the warmth
inside the house and the snowy night outside.*

*It is easy to imagine the family indoors busy
wrapping presents and trying to persuade excited
children to go to sleep. Outside the window a fat
snowman complete with a battered old top hat and
scarf, peers in at the festivities. A tartan border
gives an extra rich look to this lovely picture which
will become a family favourite and be brought out
every year when it's time to decorate your home.*

◆

DESIGN SIZE: 6½ x 9½in (16.5 x 24cm)
STITCH COUNT: 91 wide x 133 high

◆

YOU WILL NEED

* Royal blue 28-count evenweave, 14 x 16in (35.5 x 40.5cm)
* DMC stranded cotton (floss) as listed in the key
* Tapestry needle, size 26
* Mount board, 12 x 14in (30.5 x 35.5cm)
* Picture frame of your choice

1 Find the centre of your fabric by folding it in half
lengthways and widthways. Stitch the 'Peace Be to this
House' chart on pages 100–101 starting in the centre.

2 Work the design over two threads of the fabric using
two strands of cotton (floss) for the cross stitch. Use two
strands of 797 to work the blue backstitch in the tartan
border and the lettering. Work the rest of the backstitch
and the French knots in one strand as listed in the key.

3 When you have completed the stitching, press your
work and prepare it for framing (see page 126).

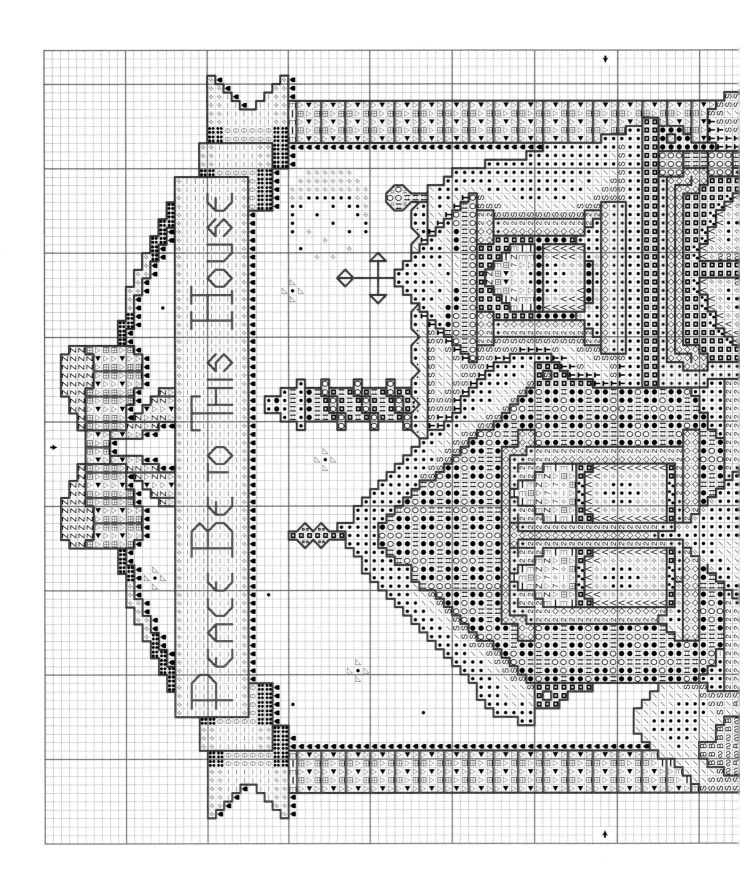

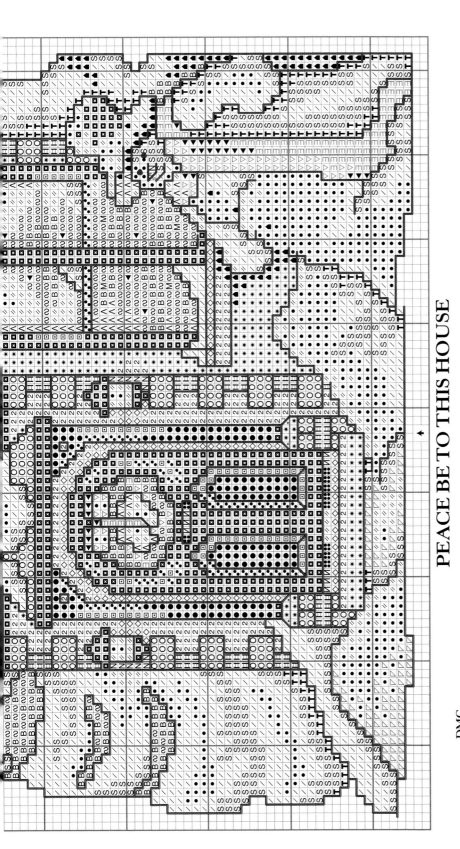

PEACE BE TO THIS HOUSE

STITCH NOTES

Stitched over two threads on 28-count evenweave using two strands for cross stitch throughout. Blue backstitch in two strands; brown backstitch in one strand. French knots in one strand.

DMC

Cross stitch

·	01	White
▼	349	Peach - dk
▷	351	Peach
●	434	Brown Golden - lt
⊡	435	Brown Golden - v lt
M	553	Violet
−	699	Christmas Green - v dk
Z	701	Christmas Green - med
⊠	703	Christmas Green - v lt
7	704	Christmas Green - ultra lt
−	712	Cream
Λ	725	Topaz
⊘	727	Topaz - v lt
θ	738	Tan - v lt
И	782	Topaz - dk
T	798	Delft Blue - dk
S	799	Delft Blue - med
▽	800	Delft Blue - pale
●	801	Coffee Brown - dk
⊞	817	Coral Red - v dk
◀	823	Navy Blue - dk
H	918	Red Copper - dk
O	921	Copper
N	922	Copper - lt
2	3041	Silver Plum - med
◇	3042	Silver Plum - lt
B	3345	Yellow Green - v dk
⊠	3347	Yellow Green - med
⊡	3371	Black Brown
∗	3740	Silver Plum - dk
▷	3747	Blue Violet - v lt
⊞	3820	Straw - dk

Backstitch

	838	Beige Brown - v dk
	797	Royal Blue

French knots

●	823	Navy Blue - dk

Home for the Holidays

I love drawing houses because I'm fascinated by all the different styles of architecture that can be included on a simple dwelling. My particular favourite is the style of house built in the Victorian period with its gothic gables, turrets and stained-glass windows. So I designed four pretty Victorian Villas in a wintry setting. This gave me the chance to use subtle colour changes to make the window bays and porches look three-dimensional. I have made my designs very versatile so they can be used in many different ways. Stitch them all together to make a lovely framed picture or use them individually to make cards, tree decorations, or to decorate a willow wreath. You could also sew them in the corner of a table napkin, using waste canvas, or stitch all four to go in coasters. However you decide to use them, I'm sure these houses will add a lovely homely touch in the festive season.

◆

The Framed Picture

Stitched together, the four houses make a lovely picture to hang up during the festive season.

◆

DESIGN SIZE: 5⅞ x 7⅞in (15 x 20cm)
STITCH COUNT: 83 wide x 111 high

◆

YOU WILL NEED

• Ice blue 28-count evenweave, 12 x 14in (30.5 x 35.5cm)
• DMC stranded cotton (floss) as listed in the key
• Kreinik Blending Filament, Shade 091, Star yellow; Shade 032, Confetti
• Tapestry needle, size 26
• Beading needle
• DMC seed beads, V4.02.666, Scarlet red
• Mount board, 10 x 12in (25.5 x 30.5cm)
• Picture frame of your choice

1 Find the centre of your fabric by folding it in half lengthways and widthways. Starting in the centre, stitch the Home for the Holidays chart on page 104.

2 Work the design over two threads of the fabric using two strands of cotton (floss) for the cross stitch and one strand for all the backstitch including the lettering. Where blending filament is required, use two strands of stranded cotton (floss) as listed in the key combined with one strand of the filament.

3 When you have completed all the stitching, wash and press your work and prepare it for framing (see page 126). A professional framer will be able to cut a shaped mount like the one shown in the photograph.

◆

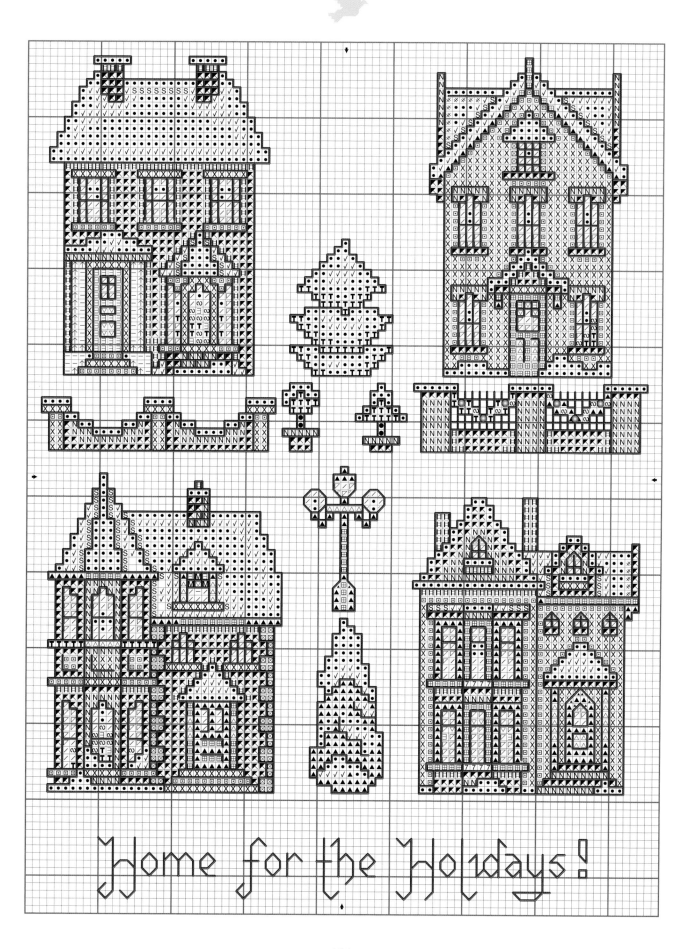

Home for the Holidays!

Hanging Decorations

Make lovely padded decorations trimmed with silver cord and a tassel to hang on your tree.

YOU WILL NEED

For each decoration:

- Silver lurex 28-count evenweave, 6 x 6in (15 x 15cm)
- Backing fabric, 6 x 6in (15 x 15cm)
- DMC stranded cotton (floss) as listed in the key
- Tapestry needle, size 26
- Silver cord, 18in (46cm)
- Narrow white ribbon for hanging, 5in (12.5cm)
- Tassel (optional)
- Small amount of filling

1 Find the centre of your fabric in the usual way. Choose which house you want to stitch from the chart opposite. Count how many stitches both wide and high the house is, and divide each measurement in half to find the centre. Begin stitching from here. You may find it useful to photocopy the chart and draw in the borders of this new chart and its centre point to stitch from.

2 Work the design over two threads of the fabric using two strands of cotton (floss) for the cross stitch (adding one strand of blending filament where indicated) and one strand for the backstitch outlining.

3 When you have completed all the stitching, cut the evenweave 1in (2.5cm) away from the edge of the design. Cut the backing fabric to the same size.

4 Fold the narrow ribbon in half and pin it to the right side of the stitching with the loop pointing towards the centre. With right sides together place the front over the backing and pin and sew a ¼in (6mm) seam all round the edges, leaving an opening at the bottom for turning.

5 Trim the corners, turn the right way and stuff with the filling. Sew up the opening. Sew the cord around the decoration, tucking the ends in the middle of the bottom edge and securing with a few stitches. Sew on the tassel.

HOME FOR THE HOLIDAYS

DMC

Cross stitch

Symbol	No.	Colour
· / ·	01	White +
		Kreinik BF032 Confetti (1)
▽ / ▽	351	Peach
M / M	553	Violet
▲ / ▲	699	Christmas Green - v dk
⊞ / ⊞	701	Christmas Green - med
△ / △	703	Christmas Green - v lt
7 / 7	704	Christmas Green - ultra lt
- / -	712	Cream
▨ / ▨	725	Topaz +
		Kreinik BF091 Star Yellow (1)
⊿ / ⊿	727	Topaz - v lt +
		Kreinik BF091 Star Yellow (1)
↑ / ↑	738	Tan - v lt
S / S	799	Delft Blue - med
√ / √	800	Delft Blue - pale
● / ●	3371	Black Brown
⊟ / ⊟	817	Coral Red - v dk
H / H	918	Red Copper - dk
◿ / ◿	921	Copper
N / N	922	Copper - lt
⊡ / ⊡	3041	Silver Plum - med
T / T	3345	Yellow Green - v dk
∞ / ∞	3347	Yellow Green - med
⊠ / ⊠	3740	Silver Plum - dk
✕ / ✕	3747	Blue Violet - v lt

Backstitch

Symbol	No.	Colour
——	838	Beige Brown - v dk

Beads

- DMC seed beads, V4.02.666 - Scarlet Red

STITCH NOTES

Stitched over two threads on 28-count evenweave using two strands for cross stitch throughout. Add one strand of blending filament where indicated. Backstitch in one strand.

Willow Wreath

Stitch one of the houses to go in a natural willow wreath adorned with one of the trees stitched on a red applique heart. A tartan bow and three brass sleigh bells add the perfect finishing touches.

◆

YOU WILL NEED

* Gold 25-count lurex evenweave, 14 x 14in (35.5 x 35.5cm)
* Red 14-count aida applique heart (Zweigart)
* Stranded cotton (floss) as listed in the key
* Tapestry needle, size 26
* Natural unpeeled wood willow wreath, 10in (25cm) diameter (Panduro Hobby, see page 127)
* Foam-core mount board, 10in (25cm) diameter
* Hot glue gun
* Satin two-colour ribbon, 1½in (4cm) wide, 30in (76cm)
* Red tartan ribbon, 24in (61cm)
* Narrow red ribbon
* Three brass sleigh bells
* Tiny gold sequins and an enamel crescent-moon charm

1 Find the centre of the lurex fabric and stitch your chosen house from the chart on page 104, starting in the centre (see step 1, page 105). Work the design over two threads using two strands for the cross stitch (add one strand of blending filament where indicated) and one strand for the backstitch. Find the centre of the red heart applique and stitch the tree on it, starting in its centre and using the same number of strands.

2 When you have completed the stitching, add the sequins and charm with matching cotton, press your work and prepare it for framing (see page 126). You will probably find it easier to use self-adhesive mount board or double-sided tape rather than lace it to the circle.

3 Find the flatter side of your wreath (they can be quite irregular because they are hand-woven) for the back. Wind the two-colour ribbon around the wreath securing the ends on the wrong side with double-sided tape. Attach the mounted design to the back of the wreath with a hot glue gun and leave to dry.

4 Tie the tartan ribbon in a bow and secure the red heart applique to the centre with a few stitches. Thread narrow ribbon through the sleigh bells and attach this to the bow. Sew the bow to the wreath with strong thread.

Other Project Ideas

There are many other ways you can use these houses. You will see from the chart that I have also included some walls, trees and an ornate street lamp to help you create your own unique projects. Simply add these motifs wherever you have a space to fill or as a trimming, like my applique heart. Why not stitch the houses in a row with the walls and street lamps in between? Or enlarge your favourite house by sewing it on a lower-count fabric to make a lovely picture. I stitched one on vinylweave to decorate a mug – perfect for your Christmas Eve cocoa or for Santa's welcome drink! There are so many different possibilities. You will find full directions on how to chart your own designs on page 126.

◆

A Gaelic Blessing

Deep peace of the running wave to you,
Deep peace of the flowing air to you,
Deep peace of the quiet earth to you,
Deep peace of the waiting shepherds to you,
Deep peace of the Son of Peace to you.

*Twisting, intertwined Celtic borders and a
flowing Gaelic-style script make this Nativity Scene
a design with definite appeal for experienced
stitchers. I decided a Celtic border perfectly matched
the Gaelic origins of this simple message of peace.
The complex knot patterns are filled in with deep
glowing colours – terracotta, emerald greens and
blue – because I wanted to recreate the look of
ancient manuscripts such as the Lindisfarne gospels.
The borders also contain the characteristic stylised
birds and animals of the originals.
Drawn in simple silhouette, the waiting shepherd
makes a powerful centrepoint for the design. The
warmth of both the design and the verse seemed just
right to include in the Winter section. And what
better way to pass a cold night than by settling
down with a challenging piece of cross stitch.*

◆

*This beautiful Gaelic Nativity design, stitched in rich colours and
embellished with gold threads, lends itself to many other projects
as well as the framed picture and bell-pull shown here. Stitch the
nativity scene on its own for a Christmas card, or one of the
illuminated letters to go in a gift tag. And the border, stitched as
far as the central diamond, would make a lovely bookmark for a
Bible. You could also stitch the word 'Peace' along a length of
aida band to hang above your fireplace, or use the border to
decorate your own padded photograph frame or mirror.*

The Framed Picture

An ornate gold frame sets off the rich colours in this Gaelic Blessing Nativity Scene beautifully. Count the squares carefully to keep your place on this complex, yet immensely rewarding, chart.

◆

DESIGN SIZE: 8⅞ x 11½in (22.5 x 29cm)
STITCH COUNT: 124 wide x 161 high

◆

YOU WILL NEED

• Stone or natural 28-count evenweave, 15 x 18in
(38 x 46cm)
• DMC stranded cotton (floss) as listed in the key
• Tapestry needle, size 26
• DMC seed beads, V2.08.3820, Antique gold
• Kreinik Fine Braid No. 8 – Shade 221, Antique gold
• Mount board, 13 x 16in (33 x 40.5cm)
• Picture frame of your choice

1 Find the centre of your fabric by folding it in half lengthways and widthways. Mark each fold with a line of tacking (basting) stitches if desired. Stitch the Gaelic Blessing chart on pages 112–113, starting from the centre. Work the design over two threads using two strands of cotton (floss) for the cross stitch and one strand for the backstitch outlining and lettering.

2 When you have completed all the stitching, add the antique gold beads over the top of the lettering (see page 125) using matching cotton. Wash and press your work and prepare it for framing (see page 126).

TIP

IF YOU LIKE WORKING ON LINEN, SUBSTITUTE IT FOR EVENWEAVE TO GIVE THIS DESIGN AN AGED LOOK. AIDA IS NOT RECOMMENDED BECAUSE OF THE MANY FRACTIONAL STITCHES IN THIS CHART.

Gaelic Blessing Bell-Pull

Mounted on a backing of stunning emerald green silk and trimmed with gold silk cord and tassels, this sumptuous bell-pull will make a very special Christmas decoration.

◆

DESIGN SIZE: 4½ x 9⅞in (11.5 x 25cm)
STITCH COUNT: 64 wide x 139 high

◆

YOU WILL NEED

* Stone or parchment 28-count evenweave, 10 x 15in (25.5 x 38cm)
* Silk or damask fabric for backing, 15 x 20in (38 x 51cm)
* DMC stranded cotton (floss) as listed in the key
* Tapestry needle, size 26
* DMC beads, V2.08.3820, Antique gold
* Bell-pull, 8in (20cm)
* Two gold tassels
* Gold silk cord, 39in (1m)

1 Find the centre of your fabric in the usual way. This design combines the left- and right-hand borders of the main project with the illuminated letters spelling out 'Peace' centred vertically between them.

2 You may find it easier to position the elements of this new chart correctly if you draw the outlines of each one on graph paper first. Referring to the chart on pages 112–113 and the photograph on page 108, make the centre of the bell-pull design eight stitches up from the centre of the bottom of the letter 'A'.

3 Position the five letters to make a vertical panel with a two-stitch gap between each one. Work these first, using two strands for the cross stitch and one for backstitch.

4 To position the borders, count up nine stitches from the centre of the top edge of the letter 'P'. This will give you the centre point for the line of stitches joining the two borders. Sew 40 stitches (20 on either side of the centre) in 783. Now stitch the left- and right-hand borders on either end of this line. Add the beads over the top of the lettering (see page 125).

TO MAKE THE BELL PULL

1 Wash and press your finished design (see page 126) and trim it to measure 14½ x 8in (37 x 20cm). Cut two 14½ x 1¼in (37 x 3cm) strips of backing fabric.

2 Join one long edge of each strip to the stitched piece with right sides facing and a ¼in (6mm) seam. Make sure that you leave a ½in (13mm) margin between the start of the design on either side. Press the seams open.

3 Place the design and the remaining piece of backing material with right sides together and cut to size. Join the long edges with a ¼in (6mm) seam. Turn the right way out and press.

4 Finish off the short edges with zig-zag stitch and turn under at the top and the bottom to form a 1in (2.5cm) hem to hold the bell-pull ends. Slip stitch the hems, slide in the bell-pull rods and place the knobs over the ends. Add the cord for hanging with the tassels as desired.

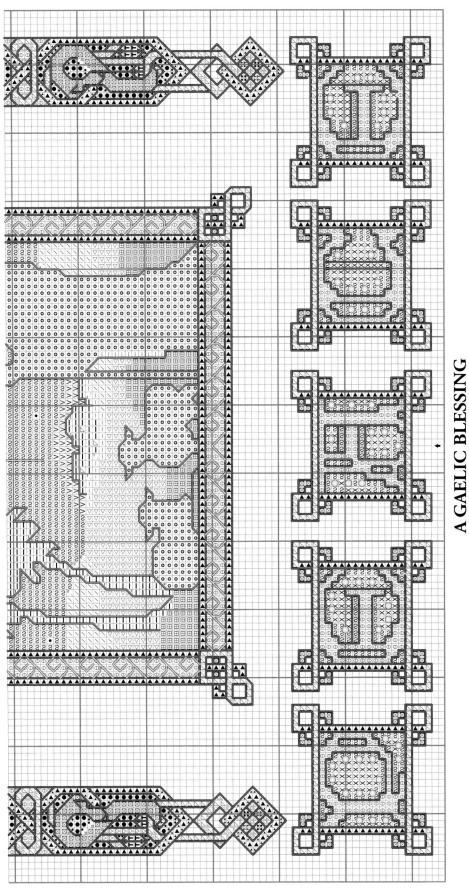

A GAELIC BLESSING

DMC

Cross stitch

·	01	White
−	336	Navy Blue
X	340	Blue Violet - med
V	341	Blue Violet - lt
M	553	Violet
▽	725	Topaz
▷	780	Topaz - ultra v dk
⊠	782	Topaz - dk
▲	783	Topaz - med
▽	794	Cornflower Blue - lt
⊕	823	Navy Blue - dk
▲	838	Beige Brown - v dk
●	991	Aquamarine - dk
9	993	Aquamarine - lt
N	3045	Yellow Beige - dk
↑	3047	Yellow Beige - lt
◌	3746	Blue Violet - dk
∠	3747	Blue Violet - v lt
⊞	3807	Cornflower Blue
T	3814	Aquamarine
−	3823	Yellow - ultra pale
⊖	3830	Terracotta

Backstitch

—		Kreinik Fine Braid (No.8),
	221	Antique Gold
—	823	Navy Blue - dk
—	838	Beige Brown - v dk

French knots

●	838	Beige Brown - v dk

Beads

○		DMC seed beads,
		V2.08.3820 Antique Gold

STITCH NOTES

Stitched over two threads on 28-count evenweave using two strands for cross stitch and one strand for backstitch. Attach beads over the lettering.

The Light of the World

Behold I stand at the door, and knock:
If any man hear my voice and open the door,
I will come in to him and will sup with him and he with me.

Many readers may recognise this project as an adaptation of William Holman Hunt's famous painting, 'The Light of the World'. Holman Hunt, one of the founder members of the Pre-Raphaelite Brotherhood, was still a young man when he produced his first version of this magnificent work in 1854. It is based on a quotation from the Book of Revelation and I have chosen to illustrate this alongside. The picture is full of symbolism. The door, overgrown by weeds and stuck fast represents the heart of the individual. No handle is visible so Jesus can only knock and await entry. Should the door to the heart be opened by the individual, he or she will be guided through life by the light from His lantern.

◆

DESIGN SIZE : 6⅞ x 8¾in (17.5 x 22cm)
STITCH COUNT: 97 wide x 122 high

◆

YOU WILL NEED

* Parchment 28-count evenweave, 14 x 16in (35.5 x 40.5cm)
* DMC stranded cotton (floss) as listed in the key
* Kreinik Blending Filament, 091, Star yellow
* Kreinik Fine Braid No. 8, 101, Silver; 9100, Sunlight
* Tapestry needle, size 26
* Mount board, 12 x 14in (30.5 x 35.5cm)
* Picture frame of your choice

1 Find the centre of your fabric by folding it in half lengthways and widthways. Stitch the Light of the World chart on pages 116–117, starting in the centre.

2 Work the design over two threads of the fabric using two strands of cotton (floss) for the cross stitch.

3 Where blending filament is listed in the key, thread the needle with two strands of the appropriate shade of cotton (floss) and one strand of blending filament.

4 Use one strand for the backstitch including the lettering and for the French knots. The outline around the halo is completed in backstitch using Kreinik Fine Braid No. 8, 101, Silver. You may find it looks better as a double-running stitch. The rays of light from the lantern are long stitches in Kreinik Fine Braid, 9100, Sunlight.

5 When you have completed all the stitching, press your work and prepare it for framing (see page 126).

NOTE
DOUBLE-RUNNING OR HOLBEIN STITCH IS WORKED AS FOLLOWS. STITCH A LINE OF EVENLY-SPACED RUNNING STITCHES ALONG THE OUTLINE ON YOUR CHART, THEN TURN ROUND AND FILL IN THE GAPS WITH A SECOND LINE OF RUNNING STITCHES IN THE OPPOSITE DIRECTION.

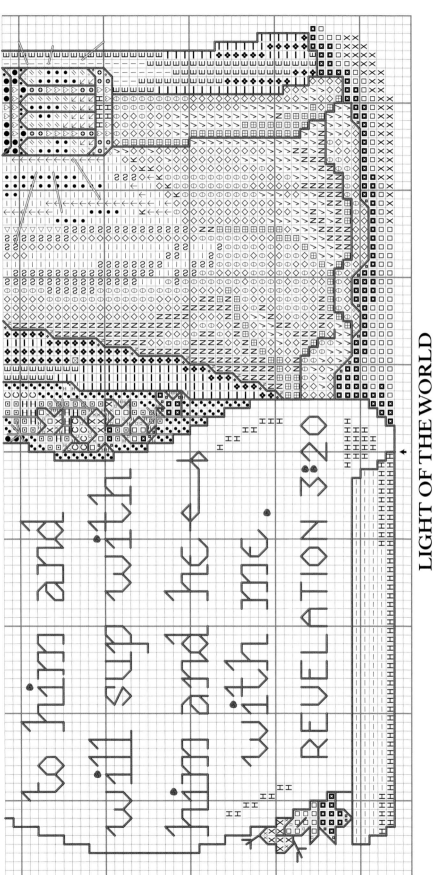

LIGHT OF THE WORLD

Cross stitch

· ·	01	White
E E	350	Peach - med
H H	433	Brown Golden - med
• •	434	Brown Golden - lt
⊡ ⊡	435	Brown Golden - v lt
□ □	469	Avocado
X X	471	Avocado Green - v lt
- -	498	Christmas Red - dk
V V	503	Blue Green - med
- -	504	Blue Green - lt
⊖ ⊖	640	Beige Grey - v dk
H H	642	Beige Grey - dk

⊞ ⊞	646	Beaver Grey - dk
N N	647	Beaver Grey - med
◇ ◇	648	Beaver Grey - lt
⊘ ⊘	727	Topaz - v lt +
		Kreinik BF091 Star Yellow (1)
⊓ ⊓	741	Tangerine - med
↑ ↑	744	Yellow - pale
⊘ ⊘	745	Yellow - ultra pale +
		Kreinik BF091 Star Yellow (1)
- -	746	Off White
T T	830	Golden Olive - dk
G G	831	Golden Olive - med

4 4	833	Golden Olive - lt
● ●	838	Beige Brown - v dk
⊕ ⊕	902	Garnet - v dk
⊡ ⊡	934	Black Avocado Green
▽ ▽	3064	Desert Sand - lt
∥ ∥	3341	Apricot
∕ ∕	3774	Desert Sand - v lt
⊕ ⊕	3790	Beige Grey - ultra dk
K K	3820	Straw - dk
S S	3825	Pumpkin - pale
S S	3826	Rust - dk
▶ ▼	3829	Golden Sand - v dk

Backstitch

— Kreinik Fine Braid (No.8) 101 Silver
— 741 Tangerine - med
— 838 Beige Brown - v dk

Long stitch

— Kreinik Fine Braid (No.8) 9100 Sunlight

French knots

● 838 Beige Brown - v dk

STITCH NOTES

Stitched over two threads on 28-count evenweave using two strands for cross stitch. Add one strand of blending filament where indicated. Backstitch and French knots in one strand.

The Never-Ending Circle

'Not until the loom is silent and the shuttles cease to fly,
will God unfold the canvas and explain the reason why.
The dark threads are as useful in the Weaver's skilful hand,
as the threads of gold and silver in the pattern He has planned.

*T*his lovely verse seemed the perfect way to end a book of inspirational needlework. Like the walled garden sampler in the opening chapter, I wanted the last design in the book to celebrate the continuity of life and love. A grandmother proudly nurses her new grandchild remembering, no doubt, when as a young woman she sang her own babies to sleep. Within her arms she holds both her past and her future, and she smiles at the slumbering babe who has a lifetime ahead of him. The border echoes the shape of spinning wheels and has the muted colours of a woven tapestry which fades from dark to light and back again. To represent the passing of time I included the phases of the moon, but you will notice as you stitch that there is no real end to any part of this design. It continues in an unbroken thread – as does life itself. I hope that you have found your own inspiration and joy in these designs. Few things offer the calm and solace of sewing quietly – especially late at night. Troubles fall away and life takes on a better perspective. In years to come your lovingly-stitched needlework will still be treasured, the legacy of your time on earth.

◆

DESIGN SIZE: 7½ x 10in (19 x 25.5cm)
STITCH COUNT: 104 wide x 141 high

◆

YOU WILL NEED

* Antique cream 28-count evenweave, 14 x 16in (35.5 x 40.5cm)
* DMC stranded cotton (floss) as listed in the key
* Kreinik Blending Filament, 001, Silver; 002, Gold;
045, Confetti gold
* Tapestry needle, size 26
* Mount board, 12 x 14in (30.5 x 35.5cm)
* Picture frame of your choice

1 Find the centre of your fabric by folding it in half lengthways and widthways. Stitch the Never-Ending Circle chart on pages 120–121, starting from the centre. Work the design over two threads of the fabric using two strands of cotton (floss) for the cross stitch. Some of the cross stitch is worked in a blend of stranded cotton (floss) and blending filament. Here use two strands of cotton (floss) with one strand of filament. Work the back-stitch in one strand except for the moon phases which are outlined in two strands of silver blending filament.

2 When you have completed all the stitching, press your work and prepare it for framing (see page 126).

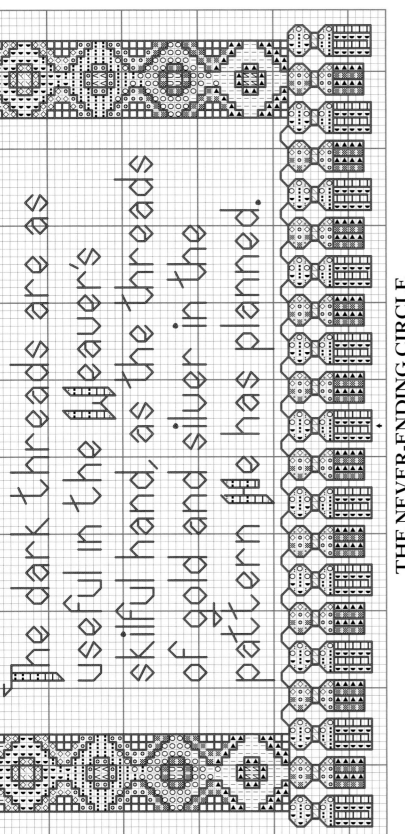

THE NEVER-ENDING CIRCLE

DMC

Cross stitch

· · 01	White
= = 221	Shell Pink - v dk
: : : 223	Shell Pink - lt
O O 224	Shell Pink - v lt
		225	Shell Pink - ultra v lt
H H 318	Silver Grey - lt
T T 340	Blue Violet - med
: : : 415	Silver Grey
▶ ▶ 433	Brown Golden - med
⊞ ⊞ 435	Brown Golden - v lt
X X 437	Tan - lt
▽ ▽ 452	Shell Grey - med
↑ ↑ 453	Shell Grey - lt
⊠ ⊠ 676	Golden Sand - lt
Y Y 677	Golden Sand - v lt
Λ Λ 725	Topaz + (2)
♣ 726	Kreinik BF045 Confetti Gold (1)
	726	Topaz - lt + (2)
✕ ✕ 726	Kreinik BF002 Gold (1)
	726	Topaz - v lt + (2)
▽ ▽ 727	Kreinik BF045 Confetti Gold (1)
	727	Topaz - v lt + (2)
	727	Kreinik BF002 Gold (1)
H H 729	Golden Sand - med
⊠ ⊠ 754	Peach - lt
• • 761	Salmon - lt
⊘ ⊘ 762	Pearl Grey + (2)
		Kreinik BF001 Silver (1)
И И 782	Topaz - dk + (2)
		Kreinik BF045 Confetti Gold (1)
∪ ∪ 783	Topaz - med + (2)
		Kreinik BF045 Confetti Gold (1)
◤ ◣ 838	Beige Brown - v dk
▲ ▲ 924	Grey Green - v dk
⊕ ⊕ 926	Grey Green - med
◇ ◇ 927	Grey Green - lt
T T 928	Grey Green - v lt
W W 945	Tawny
− − 951	Tawny - lt
◖ ◗ 3721	Shell Pink - dk
S S 3722	Shell Pink - med
▩ ▩ 3768	Grey Green - dk

Backstitch

—— 838	Beige Brown - v dk
······ 317	Silver Grey
——	Kreinik BF001 Silver (2)

French knots

● 838	Beige Brown - v dk

STITCH NOTES

Stitched over two threads on 28-count using two strands for cross stitch. Add one strand of blending filament where indicated. Backstitch in one strand unless otherwise indicated in brackets.

Basic Techniques

In this chapter you will find all the information you need to work the cross stitch designs in this book. There are details on the materials used, how to follow the charts (and create your own if you want to), and prepare your finished work for framing. Refer to this section as often as you need to.

◆

FABRICS

As the name suggests, evenweave fabrics have the same number of horizontal and vertical threads per inch. This makes the threads very easy to count, so these fabrics have traditionally been used for cross stitch and other types of counted needlework such as Hardanger. With an equal number of threads in each direction, every stitch will come out the same size. When buying evenweaves, remember it is the number of threads per inch that will determine the finished size of a project.

Most people begin cross stitching on Aida. This is manufactured so that the threads are grouped in blocks. One stitch is made over each block, making counting easy and reducing the likelihood of mistakes which have to be unpicked. The count refers to the number of blocks (or stitches) per inch. The higher the number of blocks, the smaller the design will be. For example, the same project stitched on both 14- and 16-count aida will come out larger on 14-count which has fewer blocks per inch.

As you progress with your needlework you may wish to begin using higher-count fabrics like Linda or Jobelan which are woven with single threads, rather than in blocks, to give a finer look to projects. Cross stitch is normally worked over two threads in each direction on these fabrics. For example, a project sewn over two threads on 28-count evenweave will come out the same size as if you stitched it on 14-count aida.

Most of the designs in this book use only whole and half cross stitch, and backstitch. This means that they can be stitched on either aida or other evenweave fabrics. The Gaelic Blessing Nativity Scene and The Light of the World contain quite a few fractional stitches and are best sewn on evenweave rather than aida. Both aida and other even-weave fabrics are now available in a greater array of colours

than ever before, so you have plenty to choose from. Some of the fabric colours in this book have been specifically chosen to enhance the finished design, for example, the Fisherman's Prayer and the 'Peace Be to this House' pictures. When stitching on a dark background, try to sew as much of it as possible in natural light. It also helps to place something pale, such as a white pillowcase, behind the work to make the holes of the fabric easier to see.

If a design is intended to be cut out, for example the cherubs on the mobile in the christening gifts section, stitch it on perforated paper or plastic canvas. This comes in a good range of colours and allows you to give your work a three-dimensional look. Only whole and half cross stitches and backstitch can be worked on these materials, but they are ideal for beads. Alternatively, stitch the design on the evenweave or aida fabric of your choice and then finish it off with Needlework Finisher or fabric stiffener. This will prevent the fabric from fraying when cut to shape whilst at the same time remaining pliable. In every case, read and follow the manufacturer's instructions carefully.

If you wish to stitch a design on a non-evenweave fabric like cotton or jersey, you will need to use waste canvas. This is especially good for applying small spot designs to clothing, table and bed linen. Waste canvas provides a grid for you to keep your stitches even. The canvas is cut to size and tacked to the item you wish to cross stitch on. You then follow the chart in the usual way, stitching through the holes of the canvas and into the fabric below. When you have finished stitching, cut away the excess waste canvas. Spray the design with warm water and, using tweezers, pull out the threads of the waste canvas one at a time. You may need to re-apply the water but do not pull out more than one thread at a time in case you damage your work.

◆

NEEDLES

These should be blunt and slip easily through the fabric rather than pierce it. A size 24 or size 26 tapestry needle is best to stitch the designs in this book. Like fabrics, needle sizes are graded so that the higher the number the finer the needle. Use a size 24 needle on 14-count aida or larger, and a size 26 needle on 16-count and finer fabric. Never leave a needle in your work when you have finished stitching for the day because it may leave a permanent impression or, at worst, a rusty mark.

Magnetic strips are useful for keeping track of needles, especially when stitching a design with frequent colour changes and several similar shades. Thread a needle with each of the colours and keep these lined up on the strip to speed up your work and avoid confusion.

Some of the designs in the book use beads to enhance the finished look and you can buy specialist beading needles. However, these are usually very fine and often quite long making them rather awkward to handle. A size 26 needle will pass through the eye of most beads.

THREADS

All of the projects in this book use six-strand embroidery cotton (floss). The size of the background fabric will determine the number of strands you need to stitch with to give good coverage. As a general rule, use three or four strands on 11-count, two strands on 14-count, 16-count and 18-count fabrics, and just one for higher counts.

To achieve a smooth finish and show off the sheen of the colours to their best advantage, separate the strands by pulling them one by one from the length and recombine them before threading your needle. The working instructions for each project give details of how many strands are needed to use for the cross stitch, half stitch and backstitch.

When the key lists a blend of two different colours of stranded cotton (floss), the number of strands to use for each colour is listed in brackets. For example, '744 (1) + 745 (1)' tells you to thread your needle with one strand of 744 and one strand of 745.

I also used Kreinik blending filament and braids to enhance the designs. Blending filament can add an extra sparkle and highlight parts of a design. Some designs, for example the Never-Ending Circle, are stitched with a mixture of blending filament and stranded cotton (floss). Here, the filament needs to be knotted onto the needle before the other thread is added. As the fibres have different qualities this will give maximum control of the threads while stitching.

Kreinik braid comes in a large palette of colours and has a lovely metallic finish. The braids range in size from a very fine No. 4 to a thick No. 32. They are normally used on their own to outline or to fill in small areas of cross stitch for a really rich effect.

As a general rule, you will need to cut fairly short lengths when stitching with metallic threads to prevent twisting and fraying which will spoil the finished effect. And separate the strands of cotton (floss) before combining them with blending filament for a smooth finish.

HOOPS AND FRAMES

You will probably want your fabric held taut in a hoop while you sew, although having said that, many stitchers also prefer to stitch without anything. Traditional wooden hoops have a screw fitting which makes it easy to adjust the tension. This is useful because you will probably need to do this regularly while you are working. Place the screw in the '2 o'clock' position if you are left-handed and in the '10 o'clock' position if you are right-handed. This will prevent your cotton from snagging as you stitch.

Flexi-hoops are a particularly good choice of frame if you are working on a small design because they can be

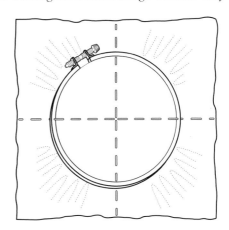

Working in a hoop

used to frame the piece once it is finished. On larger designs like the seasonal banners the finished effect will be greatly enhanced if the whole design is kept taut while you are stitching. Stretcher bars or a rectangular frame which will accommodate the entire piece are worth investing in if you intend to stitch a lot of large projects.

PREPARING TO START

As a general rule, cut your fabric at least 3in (7.5cm) larger each side than the design size, or cut to the size specified on each project. To prevent the edges from fraying, whipstitch or zig-zag them on a machine before you start. Alternatively use masking tape to cover the raw edges. Do not be tempted to use ordinary sticky tape because this will leave a residue when removed.

It is important to find the centre point of your fabric. The easiest way to do this is by folding it in half first lengthways and then widthways. The point where the lines cross is the centre of your fabric. For ease of working you may wish to mark these lines with tacking (basting) stitches but do not use too dark a colour or it may leave behind a residue of tiny fibres which will remain visible.

When you have found the middle of your fabric, look for the four arrows on the chart. Follow these lines to where they intersect to find the centre of your design. By starting from this point in the centre of your fabric you will ensure that the project is correctly positioned.

Never begin or end with a knot. Bring the needle up through the underside of the fabric, keeping hold of about 1in (2.5cm) of thread and secure this tail with your first few stitches. When you finish off a thread, run the needle under a few stitches on the back and snip off the excess close to the stitching using sharp-pointed embroidery scissors. Cut your length of cotton (floss) no longer than 18in (46cm) to prevent it tangling. If it becomes twisted let the needle dangle down and unwind of its own accord.

CALCULATING THE FINISHED SIZE

A finished design size for the stitched sample shown in the photograph is given for each project in the book. Knowing that you may want your stitching to be larger or smaller than this, the stitch count for each project has also been listed. To determine what size the design will be when stitched on a different count fabric, divide the two measurements of the stitch count by the number of threads per inch in your chosen fabric. When the design is stitched over two threads of a fabric, remember to divide the stitch count by half the number of threads per inch (for example 28 becomes 14). And allow enough fabric for your chosen finishing technique.

READING CHARTS

Each square on the chart represents one cross stitch. The squares contain symbols which relate to the different shades of stranded cotton (floss) used. Every project has a key which lists each symbol against the cotton colour it represents. One or two charts, such as the Gaelic Blessing Nativity scene, also include fractional stitches.

These appear on the charts as small symbols printed in the corner of the square. Where two different small symbols share a square, make a quarter stitch in one shade and a three-quarter stitch in the other. One symbol on its own calls for one three-quarter stitch. These are not as difficult as they sound (see the diagram on page 125) and give more realistic curves than whole stitches would.

Some projects use a combination of whole and half cross stitch. Often the same colour thread will be used in both areas but they are always fully described and allocated separate symbols on the key to help you distinguish between the whole and half cross stitch.

Backstitch brings the designs to life and should not be worked until all the other stitching is complete. Many of the designs include several different shades of backstitch to add depth. In all cases these appear in colour on the black and white symbol charts and are listed in the key.

Text is an important part of many of the projects and the instructions list the number of strands to use. Careful counting is needed, especially when stitching over two threads, to avoid mistakes. Keep an even tension: too tight and the lettering will look spidery; too loose and it will lose definition and be difficult to read. Avoid trailing the thread across large areas on the back because it will show through as a ghostly outline when the work has been framed.

WORKING THE STITCHES

CROSS STITCH

Each cross stitch is made up of two half stitches forming a cross. Count the squares away from the centre to find the position of each stitch on the chart and on the fabric. Bring the needle up through the fabric in the bottom-left corner of the square and push it down in the top-right corner. Bring it up in the bottom right corner and push it down in the top left. When working a block of stitches in the same colour stitch a line of half crosses before completing each cross on the return journey. Make sure that the top half of each cross lies in the same direction for a nice even finish.

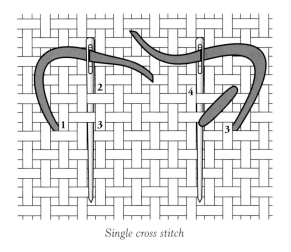

Single cross stitch

QUARTER AND THREE-QUARTER STITCHES

A three-quarter stitch is a half stitch with a quarter stitch from the centre out to one corner. It is easier to work designs with three-quarter stitches over two threads.

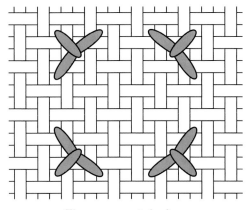

Three-quarter stitch - linen

BACKSTITCH

Backstitch is an outlining stitch that can be worked diagonally, vertically or horizontally. Working back on yourself each time, bring the needle up from the underside and take it down one square back, before coming up again one square in front of the line you have completed so far.

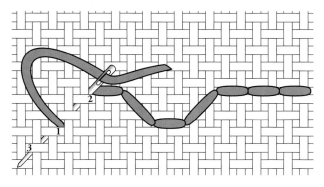

Backstitch

ATTACHING BEADS

Some of the designs are embellished by seed beads which are attached when all the rest of the stitching is complete. Attach them with a half cross stitch in a single strand of matching stranded cotton (floss) or sewing cotton. Bring the needle up through the fabric in the top left corner of the square, thread a bead on your needle and bring it down again in the bottom right corner. Sometimes I have added beads on top of cross stitches as an optional finishing touch. These are attached in the same way.

I have used DMC beads in my design making substitution easy because the many shades available correspond with DMC stranded cotton (floss) numbers.

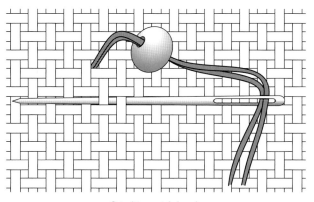

Stitching with beads

CHARTING YOUR DESIGNS

Some of the photographs, for example on page 59, are not accompanied by charts. Here, new designs have been made using elements of the main chart. I hope these will inspire you to create unique projects of your own. For this you will need graph paper (10 squares to the inch is still available and preferable to the metric version), a sharp pencil, a fine felt-tip and, most important, some patience!

Study the main chart and decide which elements of the design you want to use. Copy them carefully onto graph paper. A simple outline is enough at this stage. Double-check that these outlines are all correct before you move on to the next stage (just one square out can cause a lot of frustration later). Ink in the outline if desired and then carefully cut out the various elements of your project.

Arrange them on a fresh sheet of graph paper, moving them around until you have a design you like. Once you are happy with the finished effect, stick them in place and you are ready to copy out your final chart on a third sheet of graph paper. Either stick to the colours of the main chart or choose your own. In this case you may wish to colour in your design beforehand to see the finished effect.

You can dramatically alter the finished effect by stitching on a different coloured fabric, so hold your cotton (floss) colours against a selection of fabrics, and see which background you prefer. Look out for interesting charms, buttons or trimmings which can make even the smallest project look special. They are great fun to use and add an extra dimension to your work. Or replace some of the stitching with beads.

WASHING AND PRESSING

Keep your hands as clean as possible and avoid leaving your work permanently in a hoop. Try storing it in something to keep it clean – for example, a pillow case. If your finished work needs washing use a mild detergent in warm water. Rinse and roll it in a towel to remove excess water but never wring it. To press, put your iron on a medium setting, place the work face down on a thick towel and iron until dry. This will prevent the stitches flattening out. Take extra care when ironing projects with metallic threads.

MOUNTING AND FRAMING

Most big craft stores sell a good selection of ready-made frames suitable for embroidery, or you can take your work to a professional framer. First, your stitching needs to be stretched tightly over a sheet of mount board. Cut your board 1in (2.5cm) smaller all round than your fabric. Place the pressed design face down on a clean surface and the mount board centrally on top. Keeping the edges straight, fold the fabric over, working down one side and then the other, securing firmly with pieces of masking tape. Pull the fabric taut to give a smooth finish.

Or you can lace the work using crochet cotton. Centre the mount board on the work as before and fold over the edges of the fabric on opposite sides, making mitred folds at the corners. Lace across using strong thread then repeat for the other sides. Finish by pulling the fabric firmly over the mount board and oversewing the corners.

If you prefer, you can buy self-adhesive boards which make mounting easier. You can usually lift up the project and re-position it if you need to. When mounting a design in a ready-made frame, lift the metal prongs at the back and slide in your coloured mount board (if using) and then your design. Carefully fold the prongs back down and seal the edges with masking tape.

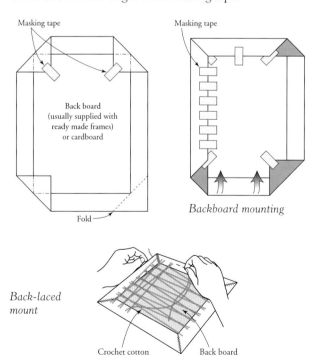

Masking tape

Back board
(usually supplied with
ready made frames)
or cardboard

Fold

Masking tape

Backboard mounting

Back-laced mount

Crochet cotton
or strong thread

Back board

Acknowledgements

There are many people who helped make this book possible and my heartfelt thanks goes to all of them. As well as my husband Ade, a constant source of love and strength, this book is for my wonderful mother and father for all the years of love, support and encouragement they have so unselfishly given me. My son Andrew and Sarah (honorary daughter) who make me laugh – even when I don't feel like it! All of you were keepers of the flame in the darkest nights of my life. And I must include our faithful Westies Anna and Dylan who kept me company when I burned the midnight oil working alone.

I would also like to thank all my friends at the Physiotherapy Department of the County Hospital, Griffithstown who have done so much to restore my strength and quality of life. Their patience, kindness and good-humoured support through many years of rehabilitation is much appreciated by all of us. My thanks go to Kathleen Guppy (Miss Beech) who supplied many of the quotations that provided the inspiration for this book as well as my lifelong love of words and writing.

All of the projects in this book were beautifully stitched by a group of dedicated ladies whose many hours of excellent work did much to enhance my designs. My thanks go to Varina Parnell, Julia Rees, Daphne White, Jennifer Williams and Lindsey Wilson. Also to Sue Smith of Crafty Sew & Sew, Cardiff who helped us find our marvellous stitchers. The superb framing of many of these projects was undertaken by Pat Henson of The Crafty Stitcher, Downend, Bristol whose expert advice, sense of humour and cups of tea made the whole experience most enjoyable.

My thanks must also go to Susan and Martin Penny who started off my career as a designer by publishing my very first efforts. Juliet Bracken who skilfully and cheerfully edited the manuscript and remains a good friend despite her red pen. Cheryl Brown of David & Charles who gave me the chance to produce this book and my friend Elaine Hammond who helped sow the seeds. Cara Ackerman of DMC Creative World who kept me supplied with miles of beautiful threads, as well as fabric and beads. The Turner family of Fabric Flair for kindly supplying me with gorgeous evenweave fabrics for some of the projects. Sarah Gray at Framecraft for the lovely mantel clock, trinket boxes and other items. Coats Crafts UK for the Kreinik and Marlitt threads which added a sparkle to my designs. Martin and Ian Lawson-Smith of IL-Soft, Witney for their technical advice and marvellous software which makes my job so much easier.

Finally to my best friends Chris Bailey and Heather Welsh who have seen me through so many difficult times. You always said I should write a book – well this is it mates!

Suppliers

THREADS, SEED BEADS, ZWEIGART FABRICS AND APPLIQUE SHAPES
DMC Creative World, Pullman Road, Leicester, LE8 2DY Tel: 0116-281 1040.

CLOCK, TRINKET BOXES, JAR LACIES, CHARMS AND VINYLWEAVE
Framecraft, 372-376 Summer Lane, Hockley, Birmingham, B19 3QA, Tel: 0121-212 0551.

EVENWEAVE FABRICS, RUSTICO BORDERS AND PERFORATED PAPER
Fabric Flair, Unit 3, Northlands Industrial Estate, Copheap Lane, Warminster, BA12 0BG, Tel: (01985) 846400.

ANCHOR MARLITT AND KREINIK THREADS
Coats Crafts UK, McMullen Road, Darlington, DL1 1YQ, Tel: (01325) 394394.

WILLOW WREATHS, MOBILE RING AND GOLDEN ANGEL WINGS (CHRISTENING GIFTS)
Panduro Hobby, Westway House, Transport Avenue, Brentford, Middlesex, TW8 9HF, Tel: 0181-847 6161.

DOG, SUNFLOWER AND CORN COB BUTTONS
The Button Lady, 16 Holly Field Road South, Sutton Coldfield, West Midlands, B76 1NX. Tel: 0121-329 3234.

ALL OTHER BUTTONS CAME FROM Hobbycraft or Craft World superstores, except for the ones on the Amish cushion which came from my Ma's button tin!

Index